SHERLOCK HOLMES'
Ingenious Puzzles

CATHERINE VEITCH AND ALEX PATERSON

For Aunt Jennifer, who is a bit of a history sleuth on the side. Thanks for all your interest and encouragement. C.V.

This edition published in 2024 by Arcturus Publishing Limited
26/27 Bickels Yard, 151–153 Bermondsey Street,
London SE1 3HA

Copyright © Arcturus Holdings Limited

All rights reserved. No part of this publication may be reproduced, stored in a retrieval system, or transmitted, in any form or by any means, electronic, mechanical, photocopying, recording, or otherwise, without prior written permission in accordance with the provisions of the Copyright Act 1956 (as amended). Any person or persons who do any unauthorized act in relation to this publication may be liable to criminal prosecution and civil claims for damages.

Author: Catherine Veitch
Illustrator: Alex Paterson
Editor: Violet Peto
Designer: Trudi Webb
Managing editor: Joe Harris
Design manager: Rosie Bellwood-Moyler

CH011584NT
Supplier 10, Date 0524, PI 00006644

Printed in the UK

Who's Who?

Sherlock Holmes: The esteemed consulting detective known for his powers of deduction and logical reasoning

Dr. Watson: Sherlock Holmes' trusty sidekick and the narrator of this book

Mrs. Hudson: Holmes and Watson's landlady at 221B Baker Street, London

The Baker Street Irregulars: A group of children who help Holmes by being his eyes and ears on the street

Moriarty: An elusive criminal and Holmes' archenemy

Inspector Lestrade: An inspector with Scotland Yard whom Holmes sometimes assists with investigations

TURN TO PAGE 118 FOR THE SOLUTIONS.

Caught Red-Handed

*H*olmes prides himself on his superb disguises and has caught many a criminal red-handed whilst incognito. Only last week Holmes went undercover as a bookseller in Mr. McCrumble's bookshop, which is famous for its priceless first editions. He witnessed a suspicious man hiding a book under his large coat, and intercepted the thief as he tried to exit McCrumble's.

"It's always rewarding when a case is solved that quickly," Holmes congratulated himself when he returned home. To celebrate, he set me this riddle.

"There were five children in a room. Agnes read a book, Adam drew a picture, George played chess, and Jane threw a ball against a wall. What did the fifth child, Mary, do?" he asked.

Can you guess?

Chasing Our Tails

The elusive Professor Moriarty is a longtime foe of Holmes. He has the annoying habit of giving us the slip, just when we are on the brink of catching him. Furthermore, to rub in his victory, Moriarty frequently plays Holmes at his own game and leaves him riddles concerning his whereabouts.

On one occasion, Holmes had enough evidence to suggest that Moriarty was the ringleader in a series of thefts across the country. Along with the police, we were closing in on the villain's hideout to arrest him.

However, when we burst into the basement hideout, all we found was the following riddle:

> Answer this riddle to find out the direction you need to follow to find me.
>
> "A rooster is on the roof of a barn facing north, and lays an egg. Which direction will the egg roll?"
>
> Moriarty.

I was ready to give immediate chase and head off in one direction but Holmes was not keen.

"Moriarty is teasing us. Let's go home," he said.

Why did Holmes want to call it a day?

All Aboard

Criminals use all kinds of means for a getaway, including horses, carriages, trains, and trams. A versatile detective has to be prepared to jump on all manner of conveyances to pursue them.

For one case, a criminal leapt onto a moving tram. By the time the tram had stopped and Holmes and I were able to board, the criminal was masquerading as an ordinary passenger, and it was difficult to identify him on the crowded tram.

However, it didn't take eagle-eyed Holmes long to spot the shifty-looking criminal, and he arrested him immediately.

Afterward, Holmes set me this riddle to test my powers of deduction:

> A tram has 15 seats, numbered 1 to 15.
> The people in seats 1 to 6 wear hats.
> Women sit in the even-numbered seats.
> The people in seats higher than 9 wear coats.
> People carrying bags are in a seat number divisible by 5.
> The suspect has a coat and a bag, but no hat.

Can you figure out which seat number the criminal sat in?

The River Riddle

*H*olmes and I have been fortunate enough to travel all over the globe in our detective business. On one occasion, a client requested our help in the beautiful continent of South America.

As we journeyed down the mighty Amazon River to meet up with our client, Holmes mused over what lurked below in its muddy waters.

"Tell me, Watson," he quizzed, "if you fell overboard, would you rather fall into a shoal of hungry piranha fish, into the grip of an anaconda whose last meal was a week ago, or take your chances being tossed over the rocks in some rapids?"

That was a tough dilemma, and I needed time to think.

Can you guess my reply?

A Case of Decorum

*S*ome cases pull at your heartstrings, and the case of Mrs. Flora Perkins, who was being blackmailed, was one of those.

We visited the elderly, distraught Mrs. Perkins at her home, as she was too embarrassed to step out of her door. She explained how a mysterious foe had been sending her letters demanding money, or else they would expose her for being seen out and about without wearing gloves. This would have catastrophic consequences, ostracizing Flora Perkins from society, since any respectable Victorian lady would never be seen outside with bare hands!

However, poor Mrs. Perkins can be forgiven for the transgression. She explained to Holmes and me how she had recently lost her husband and was dealing with immense grief. She was not herself at present. Holmes assured Mrs. Perkins that he would not rest until he had found the perpetrator.

It wasn't long before we had a list of suspects to interview at the local police station. All of the suspects denied knowing Mrs. Flora Perkins.

Holmes quickly got to the point and asked each suspect the same question: "Are you blackmailing Mrs. Flora Perkins?"

I hastily scribbled down their replies.

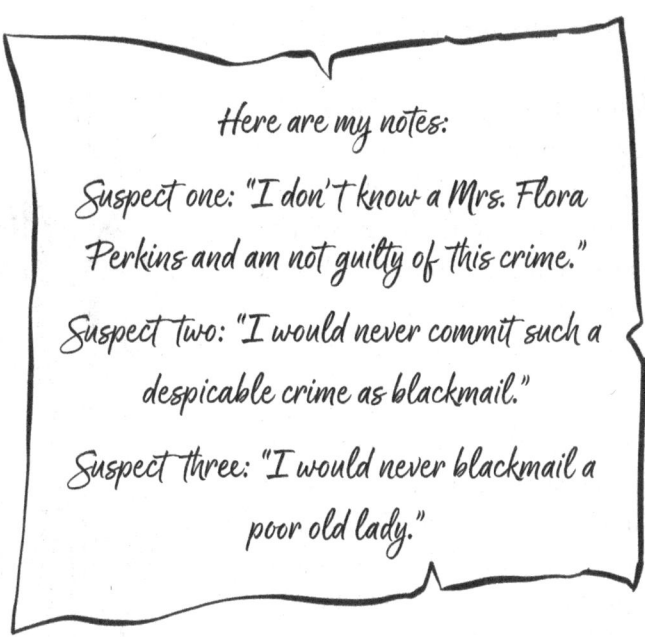

Here are my notes:

Suspect one: "I don't know a Mrs. Flora Perkins and am not guilty of this crime."

Suspect two: "I would never commit such a despicable crime as blackmail."

Suspect three: "I would never blackmail a poor old lady."

"I think we have our suspect," smiled Holmes, confidently. I was none the wiser, but Holmes was sure of his conclusion.

Who was the blackmailer, and which fact gave them away?

In Hot Pursuit

Holmes has to be at the top of his game to catch his nemesis, Professor Moriarty. Every good detective knows that a fast exit from the scene of a crime is imperative for a criminal. Likewise, to catch a criminal, tracking the perpetrator swiftly is equally important to the pursuer.

The word from the Baker Street Irregulars was that Moriarty would flee the scene of a burglary and head to Euston Station around 7:00 a.m. tomorrow morning, where he would smuggle aboard a train bound for Glasgow. Holmes familiarized himself with *The Bradshaw's Guide* to train times in order to outwit Moriarty.

He informed me that he had established that there were three trains leaving at the time Moriarty would be at the station; that the journey would take 9 hours 45 minutes; and they'd take an extra 2 minutes for every stop. And he showed me his notes:

> 7:08 train: 18 stops.
>
> 7:11 train: 15 stops.
>
> 7:21 train: 12 stops.

"Watson, from this information, we must deduce which train will arrive at Glasgow first," Holmes said, before continuing, "This will be the train Moriarty boards."

Can you figure it out?

An Age-Old Question

Our landlady, Mrs. Hudson, has a large family. We have become acquainted with them over the years as many of them have been frequent visitors to our apartments at 221B Baker Street. They span across all generations, from Mrs. Hudson's grandfather to her newly born niece.

One morning at breakfast, Holmes was in an unusually chatty mood and posed this question to me:

"If Mrs. Hudson's grandfather is twice her age, and 20 years ago he was three times older than Mrs. Hudson, how old are Mrs. Hudson and her grandfather now?"

What are the ages?

A Timely Escape

Holmes and I were called out to a farm to deal with a suspected case of arson. Luckily, the fire hadn't spread to any other properties, since it was concentrated on the barn. Suspiciously, all of the animals from the barn, including a friendly ginger cat, had been removed before the fire started.

Detective Lestrade was at the scene when we arrived. He informed us that the police had enough evidence to prove the fire was started deliberately, and they suspected the owner, Mr. Robert Parker, but needed to find a motive. Holmes turned his attention to Mr. Parker's account books, and it wasn't long before he discovered that the man was knee-deep in debt. "The accounts are the first thing to check in a suspected arson case," said Holmes. "Fires are often started deliberately to claim the insurance money!"

With another case neatly solved, as the sweet ginger cat rubbed against Holmes' leg, a riddle sprang to his mind.

"Watson, can you guess when it is bad luck to see a ginger cat?"

I had no idea. Can you guess?

Some Shameless Muggings

Yesterday, Holmes and I decided to take advantage of the glorious spring day and take a turn in the magnificent St. James's Park. As we passed Duck Island, we had the great fortune to witness our esteemed Queen Victoria and her son Prince Arthur in their carriage.

Unfortunately, the next day, a mugging in the treasured park was reported. To their credit, the police had acted swiftly and arrested three suspects: a blacksmith, an apothecary, and a milkmaid. Holmes and I were called to the station to help with the interview process. The suspects explained their reasons for being in the park as follows:

Blacksmith: "I was taking a shortcut to Horse Guards."
Apothecary: "I was in the park to pick chestnuts."
Milkmaid: "I was heading to my kiosk to sell fresh milk."

Holmes immediately knew who was lying. Can you guess who it was, and why?

The Pyramid Puzzle

*H*olmes and I were fortunate enough to travel to the exquisite country of Egypt for an assignment. The case in question involved a person falling from a substantial height off the Great Pyramid at Giza. Luckily for them, they got away with their life and a few broken limbs.

The police requested our help to ascertain whether or not the person had been pushed. But as soon as we arrived on the scene and saw the hordes of tourists recklessly clambering up the monumental pyramids, we guessed it had been an accident.

Solving the case more quickly than anticipated gave Holmes and me some time to survey the magnificent Egyptian pyramids for ourselves. It also gave Holmes time to test me with the following brainteaser, which he had scribbled in his notepad.

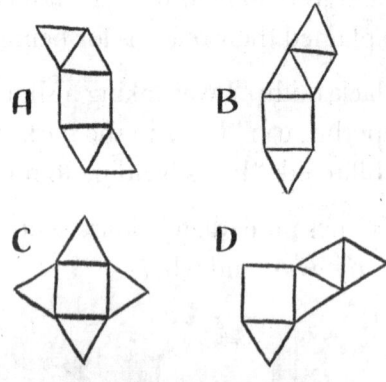

"A net is a two-dimensional pattern that can be made into a three-dimensional shape," Holmes explained to me. "Only three of these nets can be made into a solid, square-based pyramid like these pyramids in Egypt. Which net will not make a square-based pyramid?" he asked.

What was my answer?

Talking in Riddles

After some prompting from Mrs. Hudson, Holmes invited a few of the Baker Street Irregulars over to our chambers in Baker Street for some tea and cake. It was a thank you to the children for being his eyes and ears on the streets. Many cases had been solved due to vital information provided by the reliable informants.

The afternoon was pleasant, and Mrs. Hudson's cherry cake was especially well received. At one stage, though, I had a rather confusing conversation with a lad called Tommy when I asked him his age. This was his reply:

"I was 13 the day before yesterday, and next year I'll turn 16."

I could not fathom how this was possible. Can you?

The Docklands Dilemma

London's docklands are a hot spot for smugglers. Holmes and I had gone there after receiving advance warning from an ex-convict, who said that something big was happening. A team of police officers had joined us on a surveillance operation of the port.

We didn't have long to wait until all pandemonium broke out ... the moment the smugglers unloaded the crates of contraband tea onto the dock, we caught them red-handed.

It is satisfying when a case comes together. All of the perpetrators were arrested, the police had all the evidence they needed, and the tea had been confiscated.

On the journey home, I was looking forward to some peace and quiet, and a refreshing cup of Mrs. Hudson's tea. But first, Holmes sprang a riddle on me.

"Watson," he began. "Can you guess what is so fragile, that just saying its name breaks it?"

Do you know?

A Burning Question

*H*olmes arrived back at 221B Baker Street out of breath. After some chamomile tea to calm his nerves, Holmes was ready to tell his story.

"I have been in hot pursuit of three rogues," he explained. "They ran out of Bradley's Ironmongers clutching some silver candlesticks and candles."

"They ran into a windowless, dark warehouse. Fortunately, I had some matches in my pocket, so I grabbed a candle, which one of the rogues had dropped outside. Using the candle to illuminate the way, I followed them inside. I eventually found all three of the cowards clutching the remainder of their loot, just as the police arrived. I was lucky my candle lasted that long!"

At the end of his story, Holmes could not resist the opportunity to set a riddle about it.

"If I wanted the candle with the maximum burning time, which of these candles would I choose?" Holmes asked.

> Candle A: will burn for 5 hours. It has already burned for 210 minutes.
>
> Candle B: will burn for 9 hours. It has already burned for 380 minutes.
>
> Candle C: will burn for 4 hours. It has already burned for 70 minutes.

What was my answer?

Rivalry Between Siblings

Inheritance cases are not Holmes' preference, and neither are they mine, as I know from experience they can be complicated. Nevertheless, Holmes and I were asked to mediate between three brothers and two sisters from the Fletcher family, who were locked in battle for their father's fortune.

The father had bequeathed the siblings different amounts according to how long they had cared for him. The father based his decision on the fact that the caring siblings had forfeited a chance to earn their own money whilst looking after their father and were therefore entitled to a larger share. Those siblings who had not looked after their father were left nothing. And if, for example, a sibling cared for their father for 50% of the time, they would be entitled to

50% of their father's money.

Holmes explained to the disgruntled siblings that their only way to contest the will would be to prove it was a forgery, that their father was influenced by someone, or that their father was of unsound mind.

At dinner later that evening, Holmes could not resist setting me a mental test on the case.

"Watson, from the facts presented to us today, can you deduce what was the total amount of the father's fortune, if his wishes were respected?"

> Sidney: did not look after his father.
>
> Walter: spent 25% of the time looking after his father.
>
> John: was bequeathed 50 sovereigns.
>
> Iris: spent 65% of the time looking after her father.
>
> Winifred: did not look after her father.

What was my answer?

A Rectangular Problem

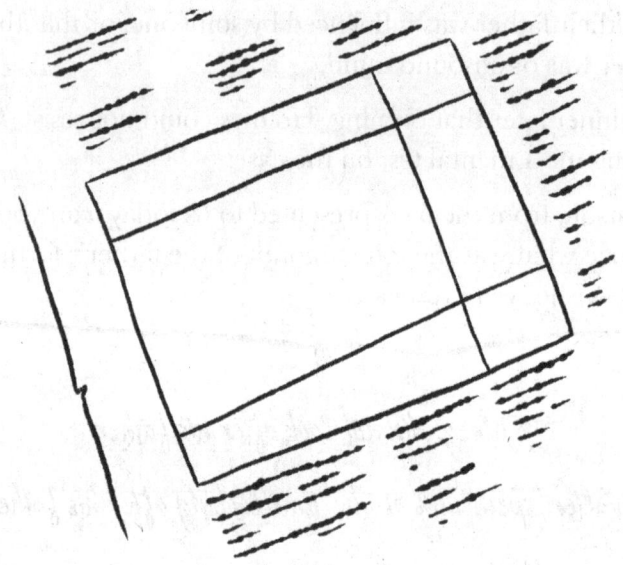

*H*olmes makes use of any spare time to boost his logical reasoning, such as on long journeys to and from cases. He especially loves the challenge of the puzzle pages in *The Strand Magazine*.

Furthermore, Holmes has the irritating habit of demonstrating his superior intellect by quizzing me directly after he has solved a puzzle. Just as I was catching up on the latest developments in a medical journal, Holmes interrupted me.

"How many rectangles can you count in this shape?" he asked, whilst showing me this page in the magazine.

Can you guess my answer?

A Coat Conundrum

*U*ndercover work requires first-rate disguises, and Holmes is a master of disguise, having masqueraded under many identities over the years.

It's rare that Holmes lets me glimpse some of his disguises, but on this occasion we were required to dress as country gentlemen for an assignment, and I needed a coat, so Holmes opened up his wardrobe to me.

There were clothes for all weathers and all occasions. As I was about to search through the coats, an idea for a puzzle came to Holmes. He quickly shut the wardrobe and posed this conundrum:

"All except two of the coats are raincoats, all except two are fur coats, and all except two are riding jackets.

"So tell me, Watson, how many of each coat are there in the wardrobe?"

I was stumped. Can you figure it out?

The Lost Loot

Holmes and I were up with the lark yesterday morning, because Holmes had received the following information from the Baker Street Irregulars about where some loot had been buried in a field.

> Stand facing east.
>
> Turn clockwise three-quarters.
>
> Turn counterclockwise by 180°.
>
> Turn another quarter counterclockwise.
>
> Finally, turn 360° clockwise.

"Watson, can you guess which direction we should look for the hidden swag?" Holmes asked.

I needed to check my compass for this.

Can you guess my answer?

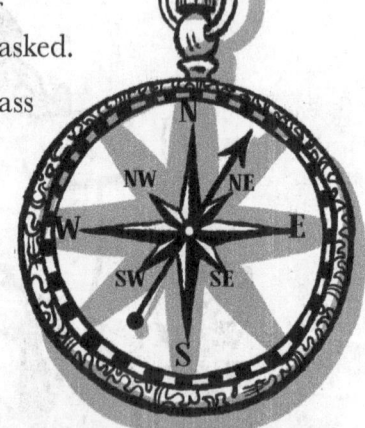

An Irritable Interruption

When we are not out detecting, Holmes and I spend many quiet evenings in our chambers at 221B Baker Street catching up on things. Holmes can be found reading over current news and events, and testing his wits on the latest riddles, whilst many of my evenings are spent typing up the day's case notes.

On these occasions, Holmes has the irritating habit of interrupting the calm by springing all kinds of conundrums on me. I admit they help to hone my mental reasoning skills, which are essential for our detective work. But I suspect the real reason Holmes likes to test me is for his amusement. It gives him great delight to see me flounder over answers that he has easily guessed.

Here is an example of the brainteaser he sprang on me one fine evening:

"Can you make an addition equation containing eight numbers that only contain 8s that total 1,000?"

I was flummoxed. Can you calculate the answer?

A Dastardly Dog-Napper

There had been an alarming spate of dog-nappings recently in the aptly named Bark Lane. Holmes treats every case with the same amount of dedication and hard work, and this case was no exception.

He meticulously studied all of the case reports, writing down the number of the house where each dog had been so cruelly abducted, in the order that the crimes took place. Many years spent in the detective business had taught Holmes that criminals are creatures of habit who frequently exhibit patterns in ways they behave.

Holmes showed me the list of house numbers where the criminal had struck:

19, 23, 28, 34, 41

"Watson, can you spot a pattern in the house numbers?" Holmes asked. "If we work out the pattern, we can predict the house number where the criminal will next strike and catch them in the act," he enthused.

Can you discover the pattern and guess which house number the criminal will target next?

A Coded Message

My writing has put Holmes and me in the public eye, and we are frequently approached by people insistent on giving their opinion on a case. Most of the time, Holmes politely thanks them, and we go on our way.

On this occasion, a passerby shoved a letter into Holmes' hand, saying that it may be of use. They had disappeared long before Holmes could question them, but the letter proved to be a pertinent clue regarding the location of some stolen goods.

Holmes showed me the letter.

> Yiu oju ulp wunf iwtr Gjwd lssc fbnh iedf nsde dppo tsd hwe eoi blpki osder ostrf tbsvc yqwse ix nw ai nq ofr lgh dnb ssjuinhc uwdfgtcv iuyhjngt Tlokimhj cjudnklo aoiknuhj swuyhjni eploimhj aj tm Boium ajuik koilm eoimn rshby Soiggy Tgyjok rdnhji elokin enhujg thunjg ledt oyhg siuj toik poilkuim riujnyhg owerfdgt pujyikui eunjhtim rhjungju toiknsfr yeijnudk.

The letter was in code and meant nothing to me. Holmes, however, had no problem decoding the letter. Can you decipher the code and figure out what it said?

Spot the Fake

Many years spent in the detective business have given Holmes a good eye for spotting a fake. This skill proved useful last week when we were summoned to Scotland Yard.

On arrival, Detective Lestrade informed us that the police had recovered six diamond brooches from a raid. Five of these were fake, but one was authentic, having been stolen from Lady Morgan recently.

The police had obtained the following description from Lady Morgan regarding her brooch.

At least three small diamonds inside.
Fewer than six small diamonds inside.
More than one round pearl hanging from it.
No gold feathers.

Holmes spotted Lady Morgan's authentic brooch, but I was confused as they all looked similar to me. Reading Lady Morgan's statement, can you work out which is the real brooch?

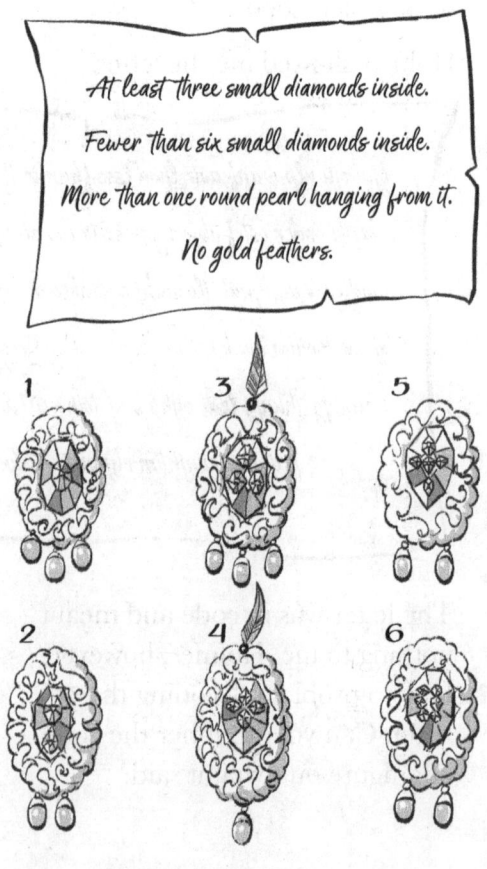

An Eye for Detail

An assignment of silk umbrellas belonging to the prestigious department store of Whiteley's had been stolen from a warehouse. Police showed us the smashed window where the thief had entered and exited. Meticulous Holmes carefully measured the space to be 14 inches wide.

Back at the station, Holmes insisted in measuring the width of each suspect. I was perplexed with Holmes' fixation on the suspects' widths, but it all made sense to Holmes, who guessed the thief immediately.

"The thief had to be narrower than the 14-inch window hole," Holmes explained. "Discover the width of each suspect, and you will have the thief."

Can you calculate the width of each suspect and conclude who the thief was?

> Suspect E was the widest at 20 inches.
>
> Suspects B and C together were 3 inches wider than suspects A and D together.
>
> Suspect E measured 2 inches wider than D.
>
> Suspect D measured the same width as B.
>
> Suspects B and C together measured 33 inches.

The Suspicious Stalker

Holmes and I were preparing to leave our seats in the Royal Opera House after watching a stunning performance of *Ivanhoe*, when an usher urged us to follow him. He led us backstage to the dressing room of the magnificent Irene Adler, one of the stars of that evening's performance and an old acquaintance of Holmes.

We found her in a discombobulated state, which was unexpected as Holmes knew Irene to be a formidable lady, an equal match in wits to him. They may have been adversaries, but they had a mutual respect for each other, which is probably why Irene sought Holmes' help on this occasion.

Irene explained that a stalker had been breaking into her dressing room and leaving threatening notes. She showed us a note that had been left in her dressing room that very evening.

Holmes compiled a list of suspects, all of whom worked there, and called them in one by one for an interview. Based on their body language, he established that one of them was telling the truth, and two were lying.

> Musician: "I am the stalker."
>
> Costume maker: "The opera singer is the stalker."
>
> Opera singer: "I'm not the stalker."

"Can you figure out who the stalker is, from these clues?" Holmes asked me.

What was my answer?

Some Light Relief

There have been a few occasions when I have welcomed Holmes' riddles. The time when Holmes and I were returning from a rather grisly murder case, where a headless corpse had been found in a Birmingham canal, was one of those rare instances. Even the rolling green hills that we passed on our way back to London did not placate me. Sensing my unease from particulars of the case, Holmes attempted to lighten my mood with a riddle.

"Listen up, Watson," he began. "What has a head and no body, and legs but no arms?"

His choice of subject matter could have been more diplomatic, but I appreciated his intentions. Puzzling over his riddle distracted me from more unpleasant thoughts.

Can you guess my answer?

READ ALL ABOUT IT

We were on a train, journeying at top speed across the Scottish Highlands. Holmes was engrossed in the day's edition of *The Times* newspaper, whilst I was watching some spectacular scenery whiz past our window.

We shared our compartment with a couple of noisy business people who were having an animated conversation about an unfortunate, recent train crash in Europe. I found the buzz of their conversation irritating and tried unsuccessfully to block it out. Ever-vigilant Holmes, however, was managing to eavesdrop whilst continuing to read. Their conversation went like this:

"Did you hear about the train crash in the Alps?" said the first gentleman.

"I did," replied the second. "Where were the survivors buried?"

I was not sure why this comment made Holmes smirk behind his paper.

Can you work it out?

The Chimney Conundrum

Fortunately, major incidents do not occur often, but when they do, Holmes and I abandon everything to help. One such incident involved the collapse of a huge chimney that towered above a pump house. There were a large number of casualties lying amongst bricks and rubble. Miraculously, there were no fatalities.

Holmes spent the majority of the day meticulously searching through the rubble, interviewing workers, and even checking the wind direction and the tides to establish a cause of the collapse.

When Holmes was satisfied that he had all the information he required, we left the scene. It was going to be a long evening, with Holmes working through his extensive notes and me typing them up. I was astounded that Holmes still found time to squeeze in a quick brainteaser in the cab home.

"Cylinders are remarkable, strong structures, which is why I'm surprised at the chimney's collapse," Holmes said.

"Can all these nets be made into a cylinder?" he asked, showing me the following sketch.

What was my reply?

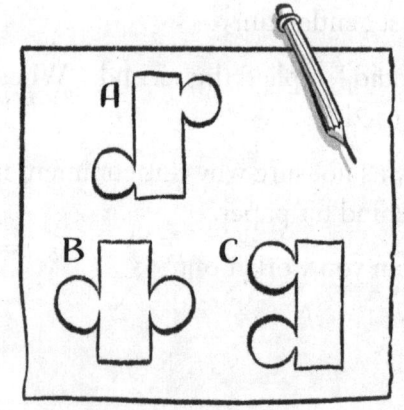

A Wet Riddle

Detective work is not as exciting as people think. Holmes and I had been trailing a suspicious-looking man along the streets in the pouring rain for several hours. We had received information from the Baker Street Irregulars that the shifty man was about to commit a crime and were eager to catch him red-handed.

I must admit that I was not as prepared as Holmes and had not equipped myself with an umbrella, or indeed a hat, and was getting drenched.

"How much longer do we have to tail this man, when he may not even commit a crime today?" I complained to Holmes, irked.

"Cheer up, Watson," replied Holmes.

That was easy for him to say, since he wasn't a drowned rat like me! Sensing my irritation, Holmes attempted to lighten my mood with the following riddle.

"If five people and two dogs were under one small umbrella, how did none of them get wet?"

I wasn't in the mood to solve it. Can you work out the answer for me?

Confusion in Court

Courtrooms are fascinating but complicated places. I am not entirely sure of the arguments at times. I have every respect for the jury members who sit there for hours, even days sometimes, and have to give a verdict at the end. A verdict that can affect a person's life.

Holmes and I were recently called to give evidence at a trial where a man was accused of murdering his wife, although no body had been found. I was persuaded of the man's innocence as he sobbed in the stand, recounting when he last saw his wife alive. But Holmes was more composed and urged me not to jump to conclusions until everyone had quizzed the man.

"How can you be sure that your wife is dead?" began the prosecution. "What if she walked through that door right now?"

The whole jury looked in astonishment at the door, whilst the accused remained unmoving in his seat.

"I've seen enough," said the prosecutor. "You are guilty of murdering your wife."

Holmes agreed with the prosecutor, but I was confused.

Can you figure out how Holmes and the prosecutor knew the man was guilty?

A Family Puzzle

Mrs. Hudson has a large family and will proudly chat about them at length whenever she is asked. I couldn't tell you much about her relatives, but Holmes is more patient than I and often listens to Mrs. Hudson's ramblings, whilst enjoying a cup of her freshly brewed tea.

Yesterday evening, I was about to retire to the living room but hesitated at the doorway, as I heard Holmes and Mrs. Hudson chatting in the room. Mrs. Hudson was off on one of her meanderings, and I couldn't make head nor tail of what she was saying.

I returned to my chamber and waited a long time until Mrs. Hudson eventually departed.

"What was all that about?" I asked Holmes, as I stepped into the living room.

"Mrs. Hudson was chatting about one of her nieces," replied Holmes. "Do you know, Mrs. Hudson has seven nieces from the same sibling, and each of those nieces has one brother," he continued. "How many nieces and nephews does Mrs. Hudson have from that sibling?" he quizzed me.

Can you guess?

The Devious Decoy

After a rare meal out with a friend, I arrived back at our chambers late one evening. I was not surprised to spot that Holmes was still up—he was often up late, researching a case or testing himself with brainteasers. But I was surprised that Holmes didn't move a muscle to acknowledge me through the window when I put my key in the door. I was even more shocked when a hand grabbed me from behind—I thought my days were up.

"Shush, Watson, it's only me," Holmes whispered, as he pulled me behind a nearby tree. I feared there must be something wrong with my vision because I was seeing double Holmes! Holmes quickly explained that he had placed a wax model of himself in the window as a decoy, because he had received information that an attempt was going to be made on his life that very evening. I was relieved to hear that he had wisely sent Mrs. Hudson away to stay with her sister, but I was concerned for Holmes.

Holmes assured me that a team of police officers was also staking out our chambers that evening. We didn't have long to wait before confusion erupted outside 221B Baker Street. In the moonlight, an assailant sprang out of a carriage and fired a shot through the window at Holmes' dummy, hitting it squarely in the head. Police leapt out from all kinds of hiding places that I wouldn't have thought could conceal a man and apprehended the assailant.

Holmes was remarkably calm later that evening, considering that he may have been dead if it hadn't been for the dummy decoy. He even managed to goad me with the following riddle:

"I'm always old, but sometimes new; I'm always moving, but never tired; I'm there all the time, but you can't always see me. Who or what am I?" Holmes asked.

What was my reply?

A Crumpled Clue

Detective Lestrade notified Holmes and me that a gory murder had been committed in an apartment building in Fulham. However, when we arrived, we were greeted by a shocked Detective Lestrade, who informed us that the body had gone missing.

The room was in disarray, showing that a scuffle had taken place, and there was blood on the floor. Holmes carefully examined the contents of the room and discovered the following crumpled piece of paper with scribbled directions:

> Go outside the building and stand with your back to the front door to face North.
>
> Make a quarter turn clockwise.
>
> Then make a three-quarter turn counterclockwise.
>
> Finally turn 90° counterclockwise.

"We must investigate these directions," said Holmes. "As they may be a clue and lead us to the body."

"Which direction should we head in, Watson?" he asked.

Using the compass, can you figure it out?

A Puzzling Sequence

*W*hatever the weather, the detective business continues, because crime doesn't stop in bad weather. One chilly December day, Holmes and I were called out to visit a client in the north of the country. We journeyed by train, because the roads were impassable. To pass the time, Holmes entertained himself with solving some puzzles in the day's edition of *The Times*.

What do you think Holmes did when he had easily finished the conundrums? He pestered me, of course!

Here is one of the more tricky puzzles he asked me to make an attempt at solving.

Can you decide which box—A, B, C, or D—comes next in the sequence along the top row, after box 4?

Kicking Up a Storm

There was a tremendous storm last night, and no one slept well. Anything outside that wasn't securely fixed was violently torn away, including 10 of our roof ridge tiles. Holmes obtained quotes from two handymen and asked for my opinion. Both were charging us for the new roof tiles and the time it would take to replace them.

"I have two quotes but suspect that one of them is trying to cheat us," Holmes explained. "Can you work out how much each is charging us and who is the crook?" he asked me.

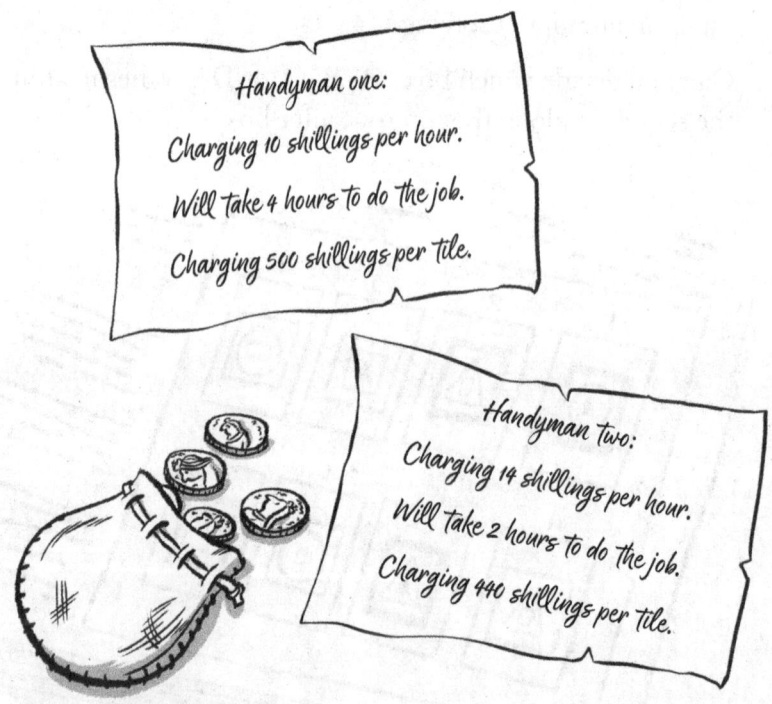

Handyman one:

Charging 10 shillings per hour.

Will take 4 hours to do the job.

Charging 500 shillings per tile.

Handyman two:

Charging 14 shillings per hour.

Will take 2 hours to do the job.

Charging 440 shillings per tile.

Can you figure it out??

The Missing Abacus

Yesterday, Holmes and I were called to St. Cuthbert's Primary School to investigate the latest in a series of thefts. It was something as trivial as an abacus stolen during an arithmetic lesson. However, this was only the beginning, and if we caught the perpetrator here, Holmes believed that would lead us to apprehending a ring of thieves operating in the school. The teacher, Miss Crawford, informed us that she suspected the thief to be one of four children sitting in the back row.

Holmes interviewed each child one by one, asking them how they were occupied during the lesson. Here were their replies:

> Frank Walton: "I used an abacus to solve an equation."
>
> Jane Howell: "I cleaned an equation off my slate."
>
> Alice Gilbert: "I copied down a poem from the chalkboard."
>
> George Webster: "I chanted the three times table."

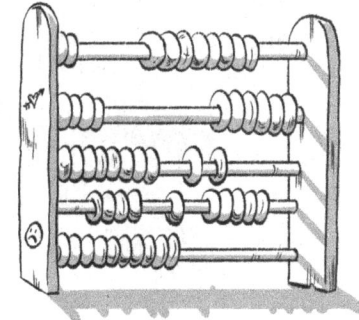

It didn't take Holmes long to establish which child was lying and was therefore the thief.

Can you solve it?

The Fatal Drop

Detective Lestrade summoned Holmes and me to a workhouse in Somerset to investigate a dreadful murder. The crime scene had been left as it was found. Lestrade informed us that a witness had seen a man pushing the poor victim out of a window onto the hard ground below. The suspect had been arrested, but he was denying any involvement. He insisted that he was outside the building and had seen the victim accidentally slip out of an open window.

Detective Lestrade and I waited outside, in front of the building on the spot of the tragic man's demise, whilst Holmes went inside. He looked out of the window on the first floor, opened it, and flung a coin onto the ground below. Then he climbed the stairs to the second floor, looked out of that window, opened it, and flung a coin onto the ground. He did the same on the third and fourth floors.

"It was definitely murder," Holmes concluded, as he rejoined us outside.

What made Holmes come to this conclusion?

The Seat Mix-Up

Holmes and I were on a train journeying back from seeing a client in the north of the country, when a commotion broke out in the buffet car next to ours. As responsible citizens, we made our way in the direction of the noise to see if we could assist.

We soon learnt that the quarrel was over a group of four seats, which included:

A forward-facing window seat.

A forward-facing aisle seat.

A backward-facing window seat.

A backward-facing aisle seat.

To calm the situation, Holmes asked each person which seat they should be in. He wrote down their replies:

> Elizabeth: "I should be in a forward-facing, window seat."
>
> Sidney: "I shouldn't be in a forward-facing seat."
>
> Bert: "Sidney and I should sit opposite each other."
>
> Rachel: "I am in the seat left over."

"That's easy to figure out," said Holmes. "Watson, can you tell each person which seat they should be in?"

What was my answer?

CODED CLUE

Occasionally, a case doesn't go according to plan. Holmes had received information that Professor Moriarty was in town, and having gathered sufficient evidence on him for former crimes, he was eager to arrest him. Catching him, however, was another matter.

We had been tracking a number of clues all over town and felt we were getting closer, until we came to this one final clue:

> My dear Holmes, you may be the smartest detective, but you can't outwit me, as I'm the greatest criminal of all-time. By the time you read this message, I will be long-gone from here.
>
> Moriarty.

In no time at all, Holmes had deciphered the clue.

"That's it, Watson, we are going home," he said.

Can you decipher the code and discover the clue that explains why Holmes abandoned the search?

A Delicate Riddle

*H*olmes and I were in a Hackney carriage on our way to our next case. I was engrossed in an interesting article on digestion from an eminent French physician, when Holmes cleared his throat, which was a sign he was about to interrupt me. He has the irritating habit of testing my mental skills with riddles, which his superior intellect can solve in seconds, at a time that suits him. I was in a stubborn mood and ignored him at first, keeping my eyes steadfastly on my reading matter! But Holmes was quite persistent.

"Here's a riddle for you, Watson," he said, ignoring the fact that I was not looking up.

"What can you break after you have given it to someone, even if you never pick it up or touch it?"

I gave him my full attention when I had reached the end of my article.

Can you guess my reply?

A Cooking Conundrum

There is nothing like waking up to the smell of a cooked breakfast on a Sunday morning. When I entered the dining room, I was surprised to find the room full of Mrs. Hudson's relatives, with Holmes reading the paper at the head of the table.

In the kitchen, a flustered Mrs. Hudson was concerned that one and a half dozen eggs was not enough to cook scrambled egg for everyone. Holmes' analytical mind quickly calculated the numbers, and then he posed the conundrum to me.

"Tell me, Watson," began Holmes. "Mrs. Hudson requires two eggs per person to make scrambled eggs. If Mrs. Hudson is cooking for herself, us, her five nieces, and one nephew, does she have enough eggs?"

Can you figure it out?

A Robbery at Sea

*H*olmes and I were summoned to Dover to help with a case of theft on board a visiting Japanese trading ship. The ship's esteemed captain, Ichirō, explained that a thief had stolen his precious watch at sea.

Holmes interrogated the three men that Ichirō's suspicions fell on. Of course, they all denied being anywhere near the captain's cabin at the time and submitted details of their whereabouts. Holmes showed me his notes afterward.

> Cook: "I was in the kitchen preparing the evening's supper."
>
> Sailor: "I was at the stern to adjust the flag, since someone had attached it upside down."
>
> Sail maker: "I was repairing a torn sail on deck."

"The evidence is conclusive," Holmes exclaimed. "It's obvious who is lying and is therefore the thief."

Can you solve the case and find out who the guilty man is?

A Sticky Problem

Holmes knows everything there is to know about bees. You can imagine how much he looked forward to our next investigation concerning some beehives on the Pendleton Estate. Mrs. Hudson was also excited, as she often used honey to sweeten our food, and had requested that Holmes bring back a jar of their best honey.

On arrival, we were greeted by our client, Mr. Buzzwell, who had netting draped over his hat. He advised that we should equip ourselves in the same manner, before he took us to the apiary where he kept his bee hives.

Mr. Buzzwell explained that someone had been stealing honey from his hives.

"But aren't we stealing honey from the bees?" I innocently asked the man.

"Bees work hard and make more honey than they need, so there is enough for us and the bees," replied Mr. Buzzwell. "I always leave some honey behind for the bees, but the thief is taking it all!"

The apiary was a considerable distance across the field from the manor. On the way there, Holmes explained to me the process of collecting honey.

"Smoke is blown into the hive to sedate the bees while their honey is collected," he explained. "It doesn't harm them since they soon wake up, but it protects the keeper from getting stung by hundreds of angry bees!"

To demonstrate, when we reached the first hive, Mr. Buzzwell blew smoke into the hive and pulled out a wooden frame. It contained no honey! The thief had struck again.

We were immediately greeted by one of the gardeners from the estate, who said he had come over to see what the commotion was about, which was surprising as we had not made a fuss. He looked disorderly, with leaves and twigs sticking to his clothes, and wore some sweet-smelling aftershave.

"I think we've found our thief," Holmes whispered to me.

What clues made up Holmes' mind?

A Riddle in the Rain

One wet, stormy day, Holmes and I were called across town to see a client in Islington.

Inheritance cases are never cut-and-dried. However, the meeting was productive since we gleaned as much information from the client as we had hoped.

On emerging from the house, a carriage raced through a puddle too close to us. I was soaked, but suffered no harm except for wet clothes and bruised pride. Unexpectedly, a huge grin spread across Holmes' face.

"That's unfortunate. But a riddle may help," he responded.

"What can go up a chimney down, but not down a chimney up?"

What was my reply?

Guess the Name

Holmes likes to spring riddles on me every now and then to catch me by surprise. He had been talking to Mrs. Hudson recently and had learnt an intriguing fact about a member of her family that he was anxious to share with me.

"Did you know, Watson, that the father of Ebba, one of Mrs. Hudson's nieces, has three children. They have been given the unusual names of Monday, Tuesday, and what do you think is the name of the third child?"

Can you guess my answer?

The Mystery Package

One evening, Holmes received a package from Irene Adler. I peered over Holmes' shoulder as he opened the package. There were a couple of tickets to Irene's latest opera tomorrow evening.

There was also the following coded message:

> Iopera aoperam boperaeing boperalackmailed aoperand noperaeed yoperaour hoperaelp. Moperaeet moperae boperaackstage aoperafter toperahis ooperapera poperaerformance. Woperaith roperaegards, Ioperarene.

"Cancel any plans for tomorrow evening," said Holmes. "We're going to the opera, because Irene needs our help."

Can you decipher the code and discover why Irene needed our help?

The River Riddle

*D*espite what people may think, the detective business is rarely thrilling. Clandestine operations can be tiresome, with not much going on. You can wait for hours for a criminal act to be committed. This was the case one day last week when Holmes and I were watching a warehouse in London's docklands.

Holmes is never guilty of twiddling his thumbs, since he is always mulling over some puzzle in his head, and that day was no exception.

"A woman with a fox, a rabbit, and a carrot needs to cross a river by boat. The boat can only carry the woman and one thing at a time. If she leaves the fox alone with the rabbit, the fox will eat the rabbit. If she leaves the rabbit alone with the carrot, the rabbit will eat the carrot. How can they cross the river without anything being eaten?" asked Holmes.

Can you figure it out?

A Commotion in the Kitchen

Holmes' expertise in logical reasoning is useful in all kinds of situations other than detective work. Last week as we were relaxing in the study, deep in discussion about a case, we heard a crash and a scream coming from the kitchen. Fearing the worst, we rushed there and found that Mrs. Hudson had knocked over a tray of jars put aside for her homemade preserve.

"No harm done," I reassured Mrs. Hudson. "It's only some empty jars."

"It is a catastrophe to me!" wailed Mrs. Hudson. "I won't have enough jars for my special raspberry preserve."

Logical Holmes immediately demanded some facts from Mrs. Hudson in an attempt to assess the situation. In between sobs, Mrs. Hudson told us that she had 15 jars, but had smashed five, and that she had made 155 ounces of preserve.

"Tell me, Watson," Holmes asked. "If there are 16 ounces in a pound, and one jar holds one pound of preserve, does Mrs. Hudson have enough jars for her preserve, or will we be eating it for breakfast, lunch, and dinner?"

A Perplexing Puzzle

I made the mistake of asking Holmes what he was looking at as we were relaxing one evening in the sitting room. The temptation to test me with a puzzle was too great for him, and he immediately pushed this brainteaser page of *The Times* under my nose.

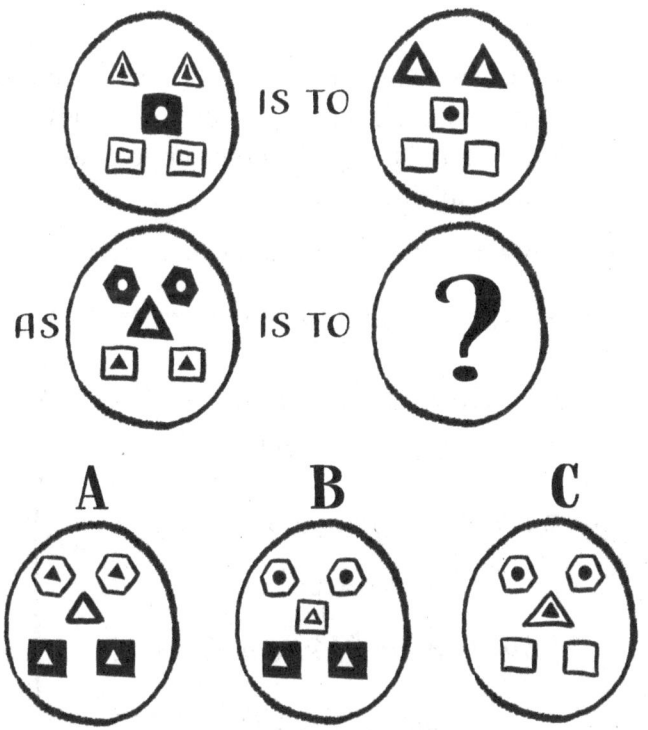

"What do you make of this puzzle, Watson?" Holmes teased. "Which circle—A, B, or C—is the missing circle?"

I admit that I was perplexed. Can you help me out and decide which is the missing circle?

Evaluating the Evidence

"When arresting a person, it's not a foregone conclusion that they are guilty, Watson," said Holmes. "A judge and jury will decide that. But it does mean that there is sufficient evidence to place them under suspicion."

Holmes narrated the example of John Grimes to me, a suspect he had recently interrogated, along with two other people.

"The evidence was all pointing to Mr. Grimes committing the crime, but I had a niggling suspicion that things weren't adding up and one of the other suspects was guilty," Holmes explained.

Holmes showed me his notes from the interrogation:

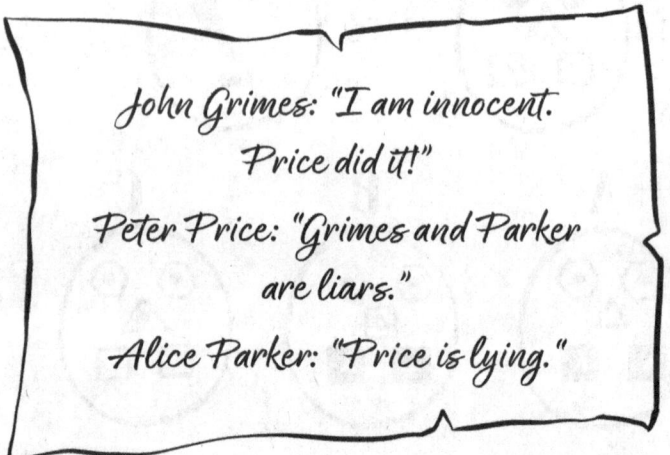

John Grimes: "I am innocent. Price did it!"

Peter Price: "Grimes and Parker are liars."

Alice Parker: "Price is lying."

"I put the word out on the streets and received this message back from a trusted Baker Street Irregular," continued Holmes.

> *One of the suspects is lying,
> and two are telling the truth.*

"I now knew who I needed to release and who I needed to arrest."

I asked Holmes what led him to his conclusion, but he insisted that I decipher the clue, just as he had done.

Can you explain why Holmes released John Grimes and tell who he arrested instead?

John Grimes

Alice Parker

Peter Price

A Royal Riddle

A remarkable summons arrived last week from Queen Victoria's esteemed royal household of Osborne House. It was a simple case of petty theft that Holmes swiftly solved. Some stolen apples were discovered in the home of the accused. He returned the apples and promised not to commit the crime again, and then he was let off with a warning.

We did not have the good fortune to meet with our gracious queen, since she had become ill. The royal doctor blamed the queen's love of pork pies for upsetting her stomach. Curious, Holmes enquired what quantity she had eaten and received this reply:

"Her Majesty ate half of the pies, plus half a pie, leaving 10 on the platter."

Can you calculate how many pies the queen had eaten?

A Well-Planned Escape

*P*rofessor Moriarty is an elusive criminal who has a habit of giving law enforcers the slip. One morning over breakfast, Holmes narrated an occasion when the fiendish foe escaped from a police safe house.

"The safe house belonged to an actor who was away at the time. It was the perfect place, as it was on an island, and there was only one way out—across a bridge. A guard kept watch from a shed next to the house, since Moriarty is fiendishly good at picking locks. The guard's orders were to apprehend Moriarty if he tried to leave the house across the bridge and to send anyone away who approached the house along the bridge. The bridge would take 10 minutes to cross, so if the guard needed to use the bathroom, he was always back at his post within 10 minutes," Holmes said, then paused to take a sip of tea.

"On that fateful day, the guard had taken a short bathroom break, and on returning to his post, he had spied a suspicious person with a large beard, wearing a big hat and coat, on the bridge. But they were walking toward the house, so the guard sent them away."

"So, tell me, Watson," said Holmes. "How did Professor Moriarty escape?"

Can you solve the puzzle?

A Worldly Question

In quieter moments I would often find Holmes studying his world globe, in order to familiarize himself with facts about countries. We were fortunate to have visited many countries for our detective business, but there were still many we dreamed of visiting.

Holmes looked up from the globe as I entered the study, and I guessed he was about to spring a general knowledge question on me.

"Greenland is the largest island in the world," he announced. "But can you guess what was the largest island in the world before Erik the Red, the first Viking to discover Greenland?" he asked.

I wasn't as well-informed on world geography as Holmes, and admitted that I didn't know the answer.

Do you know the answer?

The Missing Dominoes

I find that playing dominoes is a relaxing and pleasant way to spend an evening after a busy day of solving crimes. On this occasion, my game was interrupted by Holmes, who was surprisingly chatty. He was reminiscing over the day's activities.

I sensed that he may have been about to challenge me with a puzzle, so I jumped in ahead of him.

"Can you replace the blank dominoes in the chain with the seven missing dominoes in the correct spaces?" I asked, showing him the dominoes I had arranged on the table.

It didn't take Holmes long. Can you figure it out? The end of each tile must be next to its matching number.

A Race Against Time

There is a friendly rivalry between Holmes and Detective Lestrade, each racing to the scene of a crime to gather evidence before the other. This happened with a recent kidnapping case involving the abduction of a wealthy heiress from her house in Holland Park.

Holmes was so eager to beat Detective Lestrade that he left me to make my own way to Holland Park, claiming that I was taking too long. When I finally arrived, Holmes already had two vital pieces of evidence in his hands.

> 3E 2N 1E 1N 2NW 4E 6S 7W 3N 2NE 1W 1N 1NW

"The heiress was kidnapped from the square marked with a star, where we are now," said Holmes, pointing to the map. "The notes must be compass directions to follow on the map, which will lead us to where the kidnapper is hiding her."

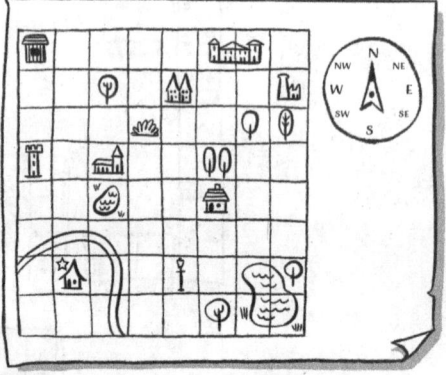

Holmes was eager to follow the directions and find the heiress before Detective Lestrade arrived, and he put me under pressure to find the location quickly.

Can you figure out the route and discover the square on the map where the heiress is hidden?

An Inventive Mind

A good disguise is an important element of undercover detective work. Holmes has numerous items in storage: wigs; false noses and ears; fake facial hair; and spectacles and hats. It is an area where Holmes excels, as he has caught many criminals whilst in disguise. He has even fooled me on countless occasions.

On the way to our next case, I decided to pick Holmes' mighty brain to see if I could learn some tips.

"What makes you so good at disguises?" I asked.

"You need an inventive mind," replied Holmes cryptically.

With the mention of inventions, Holmes then digressed with a conundrum to test how much I was able to think quickly.

"What invention lets you look right through a wall?" he asked.

Can you guess?

The Deciphering Detective

Our detective business has become public knowledge through my writings. One unfortunate consequence of this is that suspects have become more cryptic when they are questioned, because they realize that perceptive Holmes can see right through them.

Just yesterday, a suspect gave an especially complicated answer when Holmes questioned him about his whereabouts. Supersleuth Holmes soon untangled his statement, but it took me much longer.

Here was his statement:

> *"I walked into town on Wednesday, stayed there for three days and nights, and came back on Monday."*

Can you figure out how this is possible?

An Investigation at the Docklands

Holmes and I were summoned to the London docklands to investigate a recent burglary. On arrival, we were greeted by the distraught victim, Mr. Peabody. He explained that a crate of expensive gold watches had been stolen from his warehouse in broad daylight.

Holmes insisted that we question as many people as possible around the docklands. He was convinced that someone must have seen something since it had happened in daylight. It wasn't long before we discovered that a small boat had also been stolen that same day.

"It is highly likely that the thief escaped with the booty on the stolen boat and sailed along the River Thames," Holmes speculated. "It is all a question of timing. We need to establish if anyone was seen heading over to the river around the time of the burglary," he continued.

One witness said: "Thomas Evans was going to the river."

When questioned, Thomas Evans said that on his way to the river, he " ... spotted Walter Shaw, Alice Hall, and Jake Williams walking away from the river."

Holmes was confident that this information was a good start as it gave us grounds for further questioning. Who was our suspect?

A Slippery Thief

One of our more slippery cases involved taking on a client from London Zoo. On arrival, we were directed to the Penguin Pool, where we met the penguins' keeper, Mary Bright. A distressed Miss Bright informed us that one of the zoo's beloved penguins had been stolen.

"It must be one of the other zookeepers," she complained. "They are jealous of how popular our penguins are, since we draw such huge crowds, especially at feeding times."

Mary pressed us to hang around for feeding time to demonstrate her point. As if on cue, as a large bell rang, hordes of hungry penguins emerged from the pool and gathered around Mary, with their greedy mouths open for fish. Excited crowds thronged to the Penguin Pool. Penguins honked with excitement, and people cheered. It was an exhilarating 20 minutes! Whilst my attention was captivated by the slippery display, Holmes calmly walked about the area, eyeing up the other keepers.

Holmes assured me that he was not ready to jump to any conclusions yet. But he asked to speak to two keepers, whom he had noticed were acting suspiciously and not looking too pleased with the penguin display. He would also speak to Mary again.

> Elephant keeper: "The penguin keeper is lying. The monkey keeper stole the penguin."
>
> Monkey keeper: "I am telling the truth. The penguin keeper stole her own penguin."
>
> Penguin keeper (Mary Bright): "The monkey keeper is lying. I did not steal my own penguin."

Can you guess which keeper is the penguin thief, if Holmes knows that Mary is telling the truth but has his suspicions that the other two keepers are lying?

An Icy Discovery

Feeling rather hungry one evening, I crept outside and opened the icebox. You can imagine my surprise, when amongst all of the food—chicken legs, strawberry ice cream, apple pie—I discovered something that I had recently lost and had been looking for these past few days. I am perplexed how something like that found its way into the icebox! All I can think of is that one of Mrs. Hudson's visiting mischievous nephews or nieces must have hidden it in there as a joke.

From these clues, dear reader, can you deduce what the mystery item was?

> I have a twin.
>
> Boxers, surgeons, thieves, ladies, and gentlemen all use me.
>
> I have five digits, but I am not a number, nor am I alive.

Some Shady Business

Holmes and I were recently involved in a case of fraud where a Mr. Enoch Edwards was suspected of fiddling the sums in his accounts books. Mr. Edwards reluctantly handed over his books for Holmes to inspect. Holmes is a whiz with numbers, and he quickly spotted the forged entries, which provided enough evidence to convict the suspect.

Later that evening, Holmes was still in the mood for numbers and challenged me with this numerical riddle.

"What three numbers, not counting zero, give the same total when they are added or multiplied?" he asked.

My head was still swimming with numbers from the day, and I was not in the best frame of mind to work this out.

Can you help?

A Skittles Skirmish

Holmes and I were taking a stroll through our local park when a skirmish over a game of skittles broke out. Being a responsible citizen, Holmes decided to step in and help resolve the argument.

Once we had separated the warring friends and established some calm, we discovered that the argument was over accusations of cheating. Holmes roped off an area of the park, where he methodically questioned each friend in turn. These were their replies:

Lizzie: "The cheat is either me, Dorothy, or Herman."

Charlie: "The cheat is either Lizzie or Dorothy."

Dorothy: "The cheat is either me or Charlie."

Herman: "The cheat is not me or Charlie."

"If everyone is telling the truth," said Holmes, "Watson, can you discover who the cheat is?"

What was my answer?

A Predictable Case

Holmes and I were returning from a triumphant case in the countryside. Holmes had successfully deduced where a pesky thief would next strike. We were waiting for him inside the building and intercepted him as he attempted to break in.

"Being able to predict things is an important skill for a detective," Holmes informed me on the way home. And to improve my powers of prediction, he proceeded to test me on that very skill.

"How did the boxing fan know before the game that the score would be 0–0?" Holmes asked.

It would take all my powers of mental deduction to work this out. Can you guess?

The Window Message

*H*olmes has developed the rather annoying habit of leaving me coded messages detailing directions of where we are to meet. As he is so often in a hurry to catch a criminal, he will scribble the messages on any material he has to hand. This morning, he even smudged a message in the condensation on the window of our study.

I did not have long to decipher the message before it would evaporate!

Here is the message:

Step out of our chambers to face south.

Make a half-turn in a clockwise direction.

Then make a quarter-turn in a counterclockwise direction.

Finally, make a half-turn in a clockwise direction.

Can you decode the message to reveal the direction I need to proceed in, so I can meet Holmes?

A Small Piece of Evidence

*H*olmes has often drummed into me that a good detective never overlooks the smallest thing, as something seemingly insignificant can be the piece of evidence that unlocks a case.

This happened recently when Holmes discovered a small pearl button at the scene of a murder. Suspect Ivy Phillips denied being anywhere near the victim's apartment, but Ivy's cardigan was missing an identical pearl button and a forensics expert confirmed that blood was on the button found at the scene.

"I love it when we have irrefutable evidence to put a criminal behind bars," gloated Holmes. To celebrate, he quizzed me with the following brainteaser.

"Imagine, Watson, that a closet is lit by that amazing new invention of the light bulb. The cupboard door is closed, and you cannot see any light from around the door, so you don't know when the light is on or off." Holmes paused to check that I was taking this all in.

"There are three buttons outside the closet: Button 1, Button 2, and Button 3. One of those buttons switches the light on and off. The light is off to start with; you can press those buttons as much as you like, but once you open the closet door, you can no longer press them." He paused again and looked at me.

"How does a good detective figure out which button works the light?"

The Slippery Stowaway

*F*inding yourself face-to-face with a monstrous snake is not a situation I take joy in recounting, but I will retell it to satisfy the curiosity of our dear readers. Holmes and I were on board a steamer returning from an overseas case. Our ship had just docked at Southampton, and we were lining up to disembark after a long and tiring trip, when an alarming situation developed.

The steamer's cook, Ambrose Okoro, burst out from the kitchen, shouting and frantically waving his arms, urging everyone to go out of the corridor and back into their cabins. The captain, aided by Holmes, managed to calm down the terrified cook, but he refused to reenter his kitchen. Holmes pressed him for an explanation.

"I was checking through food supplies, when a huge snake slithered out of a crate," Ambrose said, trembling. "It must have stowed away on board when we left Africa. It's still in the kitchen now."

It was clear to Holmes that no crime had been committed, so no arrests were needed. It was simply a case of an accidental stowaway. Holmes had dealt with many stowaways before, but none of the reptilian kind, and he recognized that he needed to call in an expert to catch the slippery snake. The sneaky stowaway was quickly apprehended and handed over to a local zoo, where it is happily living out its retirement.

"It's always great to be of help in a crisis," said Holmes, on the train back to London. To celebrate, he set me a riddle.

"A python eats an antelope once every two weeks. If an antelope passed a python that had eaten 335 hours ago, was the antelope in danger of being gobbled up?"

Can you figure it out?

The Baffling Equation

It is not often that Sherlock Holmes, the great supersleuth, is baffled. But one morning, during breakfast, Holmes was studying the puzzle page of *The Times* newspaper with a confused expression on his face.

I was reluctant to enquire what was causing the confusion, since it would invite him to share the conundrum with me. However, my curiosity got the better of me, and I gave in.

Of course, he showed me the puzzle he was perplexed by, and not surprisingly, he invited me to try solving it, too.

"What do you need to do to make this equation true, without altering any numbers?" Holmes asked me, whilst pushing this equation under my nose.

$$81 \times 9 = 801$$

Can you solve it?

The Confusing Conversation

Mrs. Hudson sometimes has a propensity to ramble, and I often find her and Holmes having a cheerful chat over a cup of tea. On these occasions, I prefer not to disturb them and hover in the doorway, in case I get dragged into the conversation.

Mrs. Hudson's large family is the topic of many of her meanderings, since she is immensely proud of them. Today was no exception. However, I was baffled by one of Mrs. Hudson's utterings:

"I have as many brothers as sisters, but each of my brothers has only half as many brothers as sisters."

I was confused. How many brothers and sisters does this mean that there are in Mrs. Hudson's family?

A Number Riddle

We are fortunate because our detective business takes us all over the world to some amazing places. However, I have never enjoyed the long journeys across the world's oceans to get to some of those distant destinations.

On one particularly choppy voyage in a steamer across the Atlantic Ocean, I never thought the day would come when I would be pleased to be on the receiving end of a puzzle from Holmes. It was a welcome distraction that kept my mind off of feeling seasick.

Holmes presented me with these numbers:

11	22	33
44	55	66
77	88	99

"Which two numbers out of these have the same two properties?" he asked.

What was my answer, and why?

The Daily Riddle

*H*olmes always carries a notebook and pen wherever he goes and is forever scribbling down all sorts of conundrums that he finds in publications such as *The Strand* or *The Times*. He also finds brainteasers in the most unlikely places. One day, he recounted to me that his local barber was in the habit of writing a daily riddle on a board outside his establishment as a way to entice customers in!

Holmes always memorized the riddles in order to test them on me when he returned to our chambers. Here is the riddle he set me today:

"Two writers say that Percy is their brother. Percy says he has no brothers. How many brothers does Percy actually have?"

A Packing Problem

I have many friends who live in faraway places around the globe, such as Australia, Africa, and America. Many of them frequently quiz me about our detective adventures. I find the easiest way to keep them all up-to-date is by sending them copies of my books. One day, when I had some rare leisure time in between cases, I put some time aside to ship some boxes of my books to a friend in Queensland, Australia. However, it was a struggle to decide how many boxes and crates I would need.

According to shipping requirements, goods must be packed in boxes within a crate. Ten small boxes or six large boxes fitted into one crate. If I had 66 boxes to send and a greater number of smaller boxes than larger boxes, how many of each size box would I need to fill how many crates?

A Perplexing Case

Holmes and I were summoned to a home on Regent Street to help solve a baffling case. We entered the stuffy drawing room where Beatrix Price was found dead by her maid, Lilly. The windows were closed, and there was no sign of a break-in. Forensic test results had revealed that Mrs. Price was the victim of arsenic poisoning, which must have come from something in the room. The chief suspect was a decorator named Victor Leonard.

The distressed maid confirmed that Mr. Leonard had re-papered the drawing room for Mrs. Price, but that was a week before her demise. She further revealed that Mr. Leonard had decorated the drawing room previously, but to such a shoddy standard that Mrs. Price had insisted he re-paper the room for free. Mr. Leonard was not too happy. Since the room had been re-papered, Mrs. Price had suffered from headaches and dizzy spells.

Police suspected that Victor Leonard was guilty, but they were confounded, since he was nowhere near the scene of the crime on the day of her death.

"With some further investigations from a forensics expert on things in this room, I think we can prove where the poison came from and that Victor Leonard is guilty," said Holmes.

How did Holmes deduce that Victor Leonard committed the crime, and what further tests would the forensics expert need to conduct to prove it?

An Evening Emergency

Late one evening, Holmes received a frantic message requesting his help. It was from his friend, Irene Adler. Despite the late hour, we took a Hackney cab to Irene's lodgings in Covent Garden.

A distressed Irene thanked us for our prompt response and filled us in on the details. Imagine our surprise when we learnt that we had rushed over for something as trivial as a wig!

A person from the costume department had placed the elaborate creation into the safe of another performer who was away on tour. Irene sent a telegram to the performer, asking for the combination. However, the jealous performer enjoyed seeing Irene squirm and only gave her the first four numbers—8972—and a riddle for the two remaining numbers.

"I must have the wig for my performance tomorrow," fussed Irene.

The lure of a puzzle helped Holmes get over his annoyance at being dragged away from the comfort of a relaxing evening in his study, but I was still irritated.

Here was the riddle to the two remaining numbers:

Can you solve it?

> What two whole numbers have a one-digit answer when multiplied, but a two-digit number when added? List them with the smallest number first.

A Master of Disguise

Holmes is a solemn man who takes his detective work seriously and rarely makes me laugh. However, recently, he had me in stitches with one of his many disguises. He went upstairs to his chambers as Sherlock Holmes and came down as Mrs. Hudson, at the very moment Mrs. Hudson came out of the sitting room. For a second, I thought there was something amiss with my vision since I was seeing double!

Mrs. Hudson was not surprised, however, because she was in on the situation. Apparently, one of Professor Moriarty's henchmen had been bullying Mrs. Hudson to reveal some information regarding evidence that Holmes had on Moriarty. Holmes did not share particulars from any cases with Mrs. Hudson and was not pleased to hear of her troubles. He therefore made the decision to disguise himself as Mrs. Hudson to catch the culprit red-handed.

Holmes successfully executed his plan and confronted the shocked bully. Afterward, he even made a joke that his next disguise would be as Moriarty's one nephew's son's father's only uncle.

Who does Holmes joke that his next disguise will be?

THE CHICKEN COUNT

We have it on good authority that our glorious Queen Victoria often takes a break from matters of state to enjoy a simple country life. In particular, she has frequently been spotted strolling around her magnificent poultry house in the grounds of Windsor Castle.

Holmes and I were fortunate enough to view this poultry house when we were summoned to Windsor Castle one day last week, and it did not disappoint. Nestled in a beautiful, leafy corner of the castle grounds was this imposing poultry house. It looked more like a miniature palace than a home for chickens! There was plenty of open ground for the chickens to run around, and their spacious nesting boxes were filled with dry sprigs of heather covered over with lichen. The pampered fowl were even fed a mixture of boiled rice, potatoes, and milk.

But this was not a social occasion. Unfortunately, the royal chicken keeper, Mary Smythe, disclosed that she had reason to believe a thief was stealing the queen's beloved Cochin China chickens, which was the reason for our summons.

Holmes assessed that we needed to count the chickens. Before we did this, we needed to know how many chickens there should be, in order to subsequently establish if there was a chicken thief at large. However, Mary was better at communicating with chickens than people and spoke in riddles when Holmes asked her the number.

This was Mary's reply:

"If you put one chicken in each nesting box, there would be 10 too many chickens. If two chickens were put in each nesting box, there would be 10 nesting boxes left over."

Holmes thrived on a riddle and wasn't put off in the slightest by Mary's confusing reply. I, however, was flummoxed. Can you help me figure out how many chickens and nesting boxes there should be?

A Problem to Ponder

Detective work is seldom exciting. One cold, wet Monday afternoon, Holmes and I were standing on the perimeter of a pond. We were the lucky ones, as the poor police were much wetter than us, wading into the pond in search of stolen goods. An inmate from Ironwell Prison had revealed under interrogation that he had thrown his booty into the pond.

He may have been lying, of course, and wasting police time, but nevertheless a lead like this had to be checked out. All I could do was watch the wretched police pulling out handfuls of pondweed and not much else.

Holmes' mind is ever-active, however, and whilst we were standing there he occupied his brain with counting the number of aquatic creatures in the pond.

"If 65 percent of aquatic life in the pond are fish and the rest are either frogs, newts, or water snails; and there are double the number of frogs to newts, but only half the number of water snails to newts," he speculated, "What percentage of creatures are frogs, newts, and water snails?" he asked.

Can you work it out?

The Missing Square

*E*ven in the quieter moments in between cases, I can never quite relax, since Holmes has the annoying habit of springing a puzzle on me at any time.

"I have a puzzle for you, Watson," Holmes interrupted me, as I was catching up on news from the latest medical journal. He showed me the following puzzle.

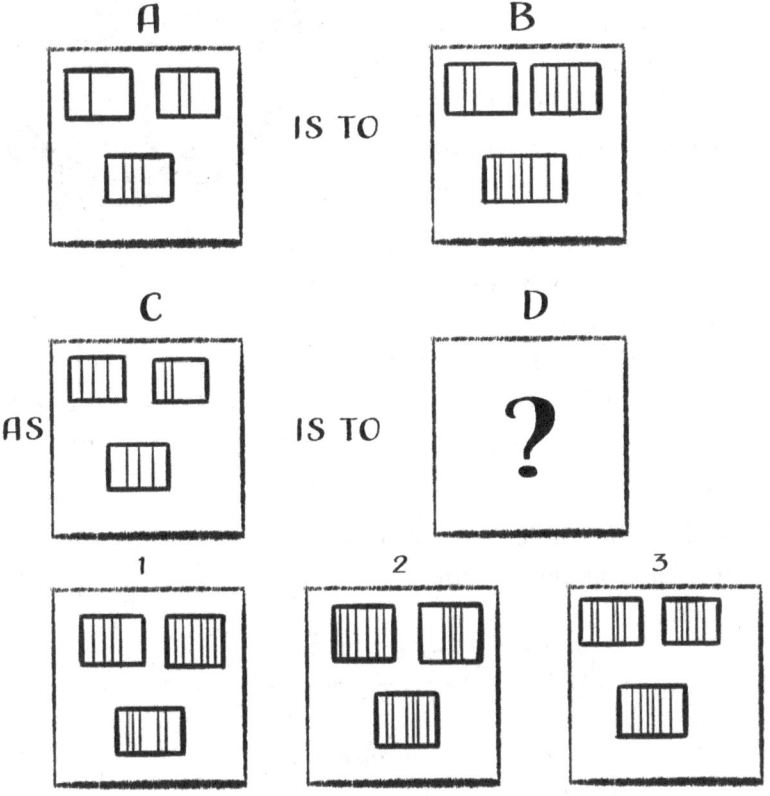

"Which square from 1, 2, or 3 is the missing square of D?" he asked.

Can you discover the missing square?

Sherlock's Biggest Fan

An especially nasty villain liked to torment his victims, leaving them riddles as their only means of escape. In particular, recently, he robbed two victims and then abandoned them at night, far out at sea, in a small rowboat. He left them with only the two oars, a compass, and a riddle. They needed to find land quickly before they perished from exposure to the elements.

They used the moonlight to read the riddle, which gave directions to the nearest land. Fortunately, one of the victims was an admirer of Sherlock Holmes and had read many of my case reports. They were familiar with these kinds of riddles and solved it in no time. The two of them successfully rowed to land and raised the alarm.

Here is the riddle. See if you could save yourself, if you were in a similar situation.

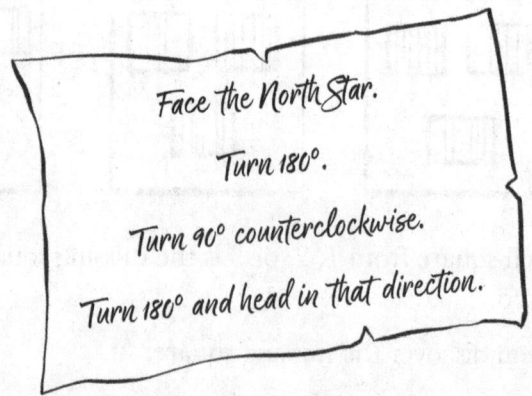

Face the North Star.

Turn 180°.

Turn 90° counterclockwise.

Turn 180° and head in that direction.

Bothersome Weather

Sometimes the weather works against a detective and aids a criminal. With one case, the pesky rain almost washed away the only evidence a pickpocket left behind. But a quick-thinking bystander had witnessed the suspicious man hurrying away and sketched a boot print he left in the squelchy mud.

Later that day, Holmes compared the boot prints of four suspects with the witness's sketch. He then challenged me to decipher who the pickpocket was, from details of the sketch and his notes.

The witness's sketch showed that the boot print had a pointed toe and no heel.

Suspects One, Two, and Three had boots with pointed toes.

Suspect Four had boots with different-shaped toes to the rest.

One pair of boots with pointed toes were the only boots with no heels.

Suspect Two had the same heel as Suspect Four and Suspect One.

Can you figure out which suspect was the pickpocket?

A Riotous Journey

Holmes and I are often summoned to mediate between warring parties. Recently, a riot broke out on the tram we were journeying home in.

We were standing on the lower deck minding our own business, when we heard a terrific thumping on the ceiling above us. We raced upstairs and found two men locked in a wrestle. Along with some other passengers, we managed to prise the bloodied men apart.

The argument was over such a trivial thing as an extra-wide seat at the front of the tram. Both the men and a lady witness had different accounts about who reached the seat first and was therefore entitled to sit in it. Holmes wrote down their replies. From their body language, Holmes deduced that two people were telling the truth and one was lying. Can you figure out who reached the seat first and should therefore sit in the seat?

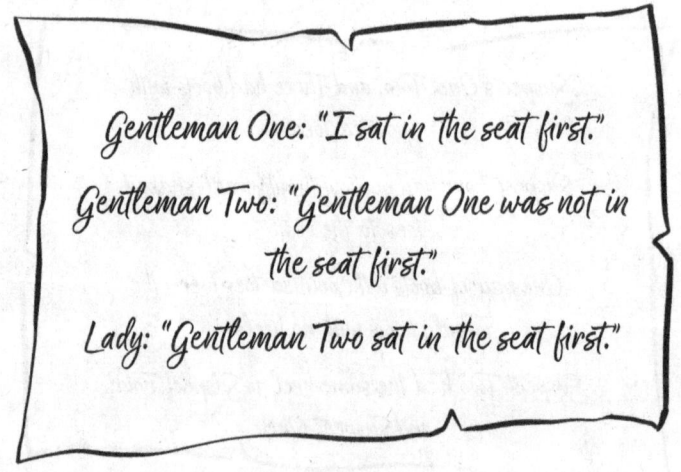

Gentleman One: "I sat in the seat first."

Gentleman Two: "Gentleman One was not in the seat first."

Lady: "Gentleman Two sat in the seat first."

Examining the Evidence

Thieves use some strange things to carry away their stolen booty. Holmes and I were gathering evidence for a case and needed to establish the object that a thief had used.

The thief was caught in the dead of night, hurrying down a street with a suitcase filled with stolen crown coins weighing 375 pounds. A witness had reported seeing the dark shape of a man exiting and entering the premises 25 times to collect coins to fill the open suitcase outside—but since it was dark, they could not record the object the thief used to transport the coins.

Three possible objects were found abandoned outside: an elegant vase that could hold up to 25 pounds of coins; a lady's hat that could hold up to 20 pounds of coins; and a man's shoe that could hold up to 15 pounds of coins.

Since it is plausible to suspect that the thief filled the object to the brim each time, which one object did he use?

Dotty About Dice

Last weekend, some of Mrs. Hudson's relatives were visiting, and Mrs. Hudson was keen to organize some games to entertain them. I made myself useful beforehand by conducting an inventory of the games we possessed. I was dismayed to discover that a number of dice had their dots rubbed off.

However, Holmes' optimistic mind turned this into a positive situation by making a puzzle out of it. Not surprisingly, he tested the puzzle out on me first, before setting it for Mrs. Hudson's family.

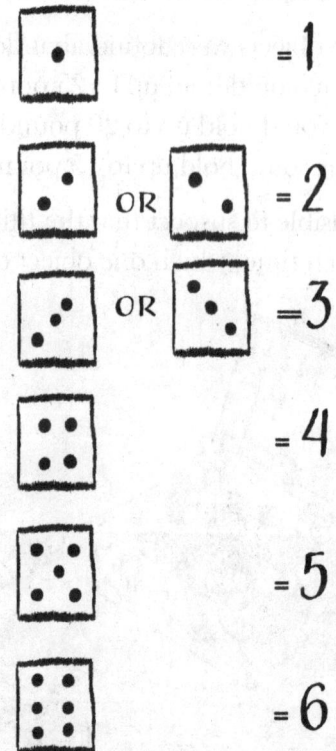

"Dice have a particular arrangement of dots for each number, so you can make a good guess which number the dice land on, even if they are missing dots," said Holmes. To prove his point, he sketched a series of dice faces with all their dots showing which number they represented.

Then he arranged four of our dice with some of their dots missing to show this equation:

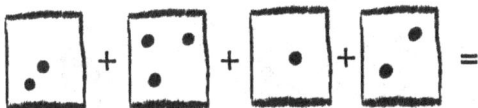

"What is the biggest value you can make from these four dice added together?" he asked.

The trick was to think of the highest number that each dice could be, and then add those numbers together.

What total do you calculate?

The School Suspect

Holmes has worked undercover in some interesting positions. His latest case involved working in disguise as a schoolteacher. The school had requested Holmes' help, as one of their teachers was suspected of embezzlement, moving school funds into his own pocket.

Holmes was surprised to find around 80 children crammed into his classroom, eager to learn. He soon realized that the job was not going to be straightforward. Holmes thought that a riddle to test the children's logic reasoning would be a good start.

This is the riddle he set the children:

"I have a box of 40 slates that 40 children need to write on. If I give every child one slate, but one slate remains in the box, how can I do this?"

According to Holmes, a few children answered correctly.

Can you deduce the correct answer?

A Senseless Attack

Professor Moriarty was an arrogant man who always left some kind of riddle for Holmes and me to find as we chased him across the country.

Recently, Moriarty's henchmen had been involved in a senseless attack on a young man. The victim was still unconscious and could not reveal any details. It was crucial that Holmes establish how many suspects were involved, so that they could all be brought to justice. Holmes soon made it known among his informants that he was seeking information.

The conceited Moriarty couldn't resist posting a riddle to reveal the number. He presumed we would not be able to solve it, but he underestimated Holmes' brilliance.

This was the riddle:

How many are there in a group of related people that includes a grandfather, two fathers, and two sons?

Moriarty

How many people were there in the group? This is the number of people who attacked the young man.

A Problem Shared

Mrs. Hudson had just returned from the market with some shopping, but was clearly upset. Holmes has a better understanding of Mrs. Hudson than me, so I hovered in the kitchen doorway whilst Holmes enquired if he could be of assistance.

"I must have dropped an apple on my way home," Mrs. Hudson wailed. "I only have 11 apples!"

Holmes and I did not understand why 11 apples was a problem. Mrs. Hudson explained that she had 12 of her young nieces and nephews coming over.

"How can I divide 11 apples between 12 children?" she complained.

Holmes glanced in the pantry and noticed that Mrs. Hudson had some sugar, flour, butter, and oats in stock. His lightning-quick brain soon worked out a solution.

Can you guess what Holmes suggested?

Riddle Time

We were on our way home in a Hackney cab after a hectic day spent interviewing suspects at Scotland Yard. I was nodding off, but Holmes' active mind had other ideas. He cleared his throat—a sure sign that he was about to spring a riddle on me.

He did not disappoint, coming out with a conundrum:

"Now is no time to drift off, Watson. I have an excellent riddle for you." And he launched into it.

"What can build castles, break down mountains, make some blind, and help others see?" he asked.

I did not care to answer Holmes' riddle since I was too tired, but it would require more effort to argue with him, so I capitulated and gave my best answer.

Can you guess what it was?

A Noisy Dispute

Holmes and I were recently summoned to a farm in Wiltshire to deal with a dispute between a farmer and a rail company. After the long journey there, we were greeted on arrival by the farmer, Cora Perkins. She provided us with a refreshing glass of cool milk, whilst filling us in on the details.

"A new train line has been laid right next to the field where I keep my dairy cows," she complained. "The noise is making my cows stressed, and they are not producing so much milk." And to prove her point, Miss Perkins revealed her accounts, which showed how much milk her cows were producing before and after the train line was constructed. There was clearly a big decrease.

Holmes reassured Miss Perkins that this paperwork was enough proof to convince the rail company of the damage their train was causing. Furthermore, since the company would not like any bad publicity, he was sure they would offer her some generous compensation. He suggested that Miss Perkins look into planting a dense line of trees with some of the money to block out the sound of the trains.

We left our client in a more elevated mood than we found her. To celebrate, Holmes set me this riddle on the way home.

"If there are 10 cows, 15 sheep, one sheepdog, and one farmer, how many feet are there?"

What was my answer?

The Mysterious Poisoning

A downside of the detective business is that we deal with some unpleasant characters. Some bear a grudge against Holmes, especially if he has contributed to their arrest. Stanley Jones had recently been released from a long prison sentence and, unbeknown to us, was seeking revenge against Holmes.

One evening, Holmes and I were invited to a party. We tucked into some delicious ham and drank some refreshing fruit punch that was chilled with ice cubes, then made our excuses and left early, before anyone else.

We later learned that a number of guests had become ill after that evening. A forensics expert established that the fruit punch was laced with a poison. It was also later discovered that a man resembling Stanley Jones had sneaked into the party, disguised as one of the kitchen staff.

With a criminal background of past poisonings, Stanley Jones was the prime suspect. I was baffled why Holmes and I were not affected by drinking the fruit punch, since clearly Holmes was the intended victim.

Can you solve the mystery?

An Eyewitness Account

*E*yewitness accounts can be confusing at times, but small things can trigger the memory. Holmes and I had been gathering evidence over many months for a case involving a nameless master forger. He had been forging reputable artists' signatures on paintings that were not theirs, in order to sell the paintings at incredibly high prices.

Nell Morgan had bought one of these paintings from a man. We invited Miss Morgan down to the police station to view a number of suspects, whom we suspected may have been the mystery forger.

Miss Morgan recognized one of the suspects as the man who sold her the painting. Furthermore, seeing him again triggered her memory, since she had a hunch that she knew him from somewhere.

Holmes pressed Miss Morgan further, and this was her reply:

"Brothers and sisters has my butler none, but that man's father is my butler's father's son."

Can you figure out who the master forger was from this explanation?

The Baker Street Irregulars

The streets of London are the haunts of the Baker Street Irregulars, where they often overhear gossip and spot suspicious things. People talk freely around them, since no one suspects the innocent children of spying. But they are a vital information source for Holmes, who rewards them a shilling a day for their efforts.

The latest information from the Baker Street Irregulars led to the recovery of a stolen racehorse from where it was imprisoned in a dingy shed, down a dark alley.

After Holmes had thanked and compensated the children, he couldn't resist testing me with this riddle:

"Watson, can you guess which breed of horse can jump higher than a house?"

What was my answer?

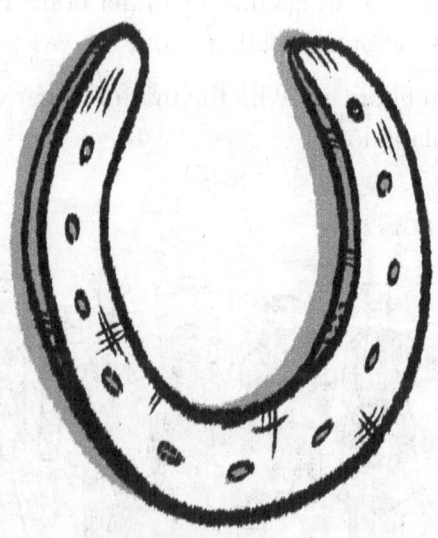

The Magic Behind the Trick

Holmes and I rarely have much time to indulge in leisurely pastimes. So when we received an invitation from a grateful client we had helped out recently, we jumped at the chance to attend Magnificent Mabel's Magic Act one chilly, wintery evening.

For the act, Mabel asked a member of the audience up on stage and gave them five shilling coins to examine. The coins were identical except for the dates, which were all different. Mabel turned her back, and the volunteer dropped the five coins into a cup. They withdrew one coin, looked at it and memorized its date, then held it tightly in their hand so Mabel could not see it when she turned back.

Mabel asked the volunteer a series of questions about themselves, such as their name, age, and occupation. Mabel turned her back again, and the volunteer dropped the coin back into the cup with the other coins.

Mabel turned back, and the volunteer passed her the cup of coins. She withdrew the coin she claimed the volunteer had selected. The volunteer said the date out loud, and Mabel passed them the coin to check. There were gasps from the audience, since it had the same date!

I was perplexed, but perceptive Holmes had uncovered the magic behind Magician Mabel's trick.

Can you guess?

The Breakfast Meeting

Holmes and I were journeying to the north of the country to help a client argue against an arson charge. We had an early start, catching a 6:30 a.m. train from Euston Station. Holmes had thoughtfully booked us a table in the buffet car for breakfast, rather than bothering Mrs. Hudson back at our chambers at such an early hour.

It had been a while since I had been out for breakfast, and I was shocked at the huge variety of food on offer. A delicious cooked breakfast included eggs, bacon, kippers, and watercress. You could also have porridge, bread, cheese, cold meat, and oranges. This was all washed down with tea or coffee!

Holmes' mind, however, was more on a riddle than the food.

"What two things can you never eat for breakfast?" he asked me.

Can you guess my answer?

Riddle Wars

When Holmes and Detective Lestrade are not out solving cases, they like to challenge each other with riddles. I try to stay out of the way when they are sparring like this, but occasionally I get caught in the riddle crossfire!

Today was no exception. Holmes was meeting Lestrade in the park to discuss details of a case and had planned to surprise him with a riddle at the end of their chat. However, Lestrade pulled out at the last moment. Desperate to test his riddle out on someone, Holmes pressed me to attend instead, which I dutifully did.

"Watson, what has two heads, six legs, four eyes, and a tail?" he asked.

What was my answer?

A Pricing Quandary

Mrs. Hudson frequently purchased her fruit from Covent Garden market. It was not her best-loved chore, because traders have the annoying habit of changing their prices from person to person. However, Mrs. Hudson was a friendly woman and had built up a good relationship with a particular market trader, someone who charged her a fair price.

One particular morning, Mrs. Hudson announced that she was off to buy some pears at the market, since she wanted to make a pear crumble for dinner. I fancied a stroll and a change of scenery, so I accompanied Mrs. Hudson, much to Holmes' astonishment. Coincidentally, it was this morning that we discovered that a new trader had replaced the trader Mrs. Hudson knew. He liked the sound of his own voice and bamboozled Mrs. Hudson with information when she asked a simple question regarding the price of a pear.

"A pear is three times as much as a blackberry; an apple is double the price of a gooseberry; a gooseberry and a raspberry are the same price as each other; a plum is 1½ pennies, which is half a penny more than a raspberry; and two blackberries are the same price as one gooseberry," he shouted.

I wished that Holmes had accompanied us, since his lightning-quick brain would have figured out the arithmetic much faster than mine. It was Mrs. Hudson who came to the rescue, however, working out the price of all the fruit, including the pear.

Can you guess her answer?

Under the Weather

Do you sometimes feel like not getting out of bed when the rain outside is lashing against the windowpanes? It had been raining like this for days. Holmes and I had been out in it, of course, since crime does not stop just because of the weather. But I was getting weary of arriving home drenched after a day out on the streets doing detective work.

I eagerly listened to anyone's opinion on when the weather would brighten, and the other night I even woke up at midnight, crawled out of my bed, and pulled back the curtains to check on the weather! Holmes had heard me and poked his head around my door to check that I was OK. I expressed my concerns about the weather to him.

"If it's raining at midnight, but the forecast for tomorrow and the day after is clear," he replied, "will it be sunny in 48 hours?"

I was not feeling fully alert at this late hour, but attempted to answer Holmes' question.

Can you guess my reply?

Trouble at the Zoo

Holmes and I were first alerted to a commotion going on at nearby London Zoo, when we saw hordes of people rushing along Baker Street, past our chambers.

Holmes ventured out onto the street to extract some details from a passerby.

"Some youngsters are creating havoc at the zoo, opening up the animal enclosures and releasing the animals!" Holmes relayed to me, as he returned inside. He grabbed his coat and then rushed out again. I gave chase, unsure of what chaos awaited us at the zoo.

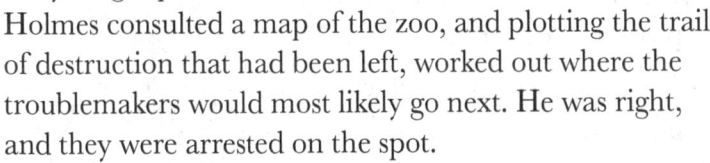

When we arrived, the zoo had been closed and the police were already on the scene searching for the young reprobates.

Holmes consulted a map of the zoo, and plotting the trail of destruction that had been left, worked out where the troublemakers would most likely go next. He was right, and they were arrested on the spot.

Thankfully, the experienced zookeepers soon had all of the animals rounded up and back in their enclosures. A giraffe was the last animal to be tempted back with some very tasty carrots.

"What lies at a giraffe's feet, keeps up with it even when it runs at its fastest, but doesn't weigh anything?" Holmes asked on our way home.

Can you guess what the answer is?

Feuding Families

*H*olmes and I were investigating a case that had ended in violence between two families—the Robinson family and the Bell family—who lived next door to each other. The argument began with a simple disagreement over a tree that had grown exponentially over the 10 years since it was planted.

The Bell family complained that the tree blocked out the light and cast their house and garden in shade. They insisted that the tree be chopped down, but when the Robinson family, who owned the tree, refused, Mr. Bell attacked Mr. Robinson, leaving him with a bloodied face.

The case was cut-and-dried. Holmes concluded that Mr. Robinson had not broken any laws, but Mr. Bell had taken the law into his own hands and acted with violence, so he was the guilty party.

Back at our chambers later that evening, ever-curious Holmes speculated about the rate of the offending tree's growth and posed this conundrum:

"If the tree was one unit tall when it was planted, doubled in height each year, and reached its maximum height after 10 years, how many years did the tree take to reach half its maximum height when it was felled?"

What was my reply?

The Mysterious Escape

Holmes and I were summoned to a jail in Derby, where an escape was baffling the authorities.

A guard informed us that the criminal had escaped from the prison kitchen, where he worked during the day. The kitchen door had a guard stationed outside during the day. The only way of escape out of the kitchen was a small window that was 5 feet 10 inches up from the ground—too tall for the man to reach, as he was only 5 feet 5 inches. Only one prisoner at a time worked inside the kitchen, and all of the fittings were tightly secured to the floor, so they could not be moved.

When Holmes searched for clues inside the kitchen, he noticed that, rather bizarrely, below the window was a large pool of water. Holmes instantly deduced how the man had escaped.

Can you solve this conundrum too?

A Canine Conundrum

Scotland Yard had received a number of complaints regarding some unpleasant smells coming from a property on Pong Street and had requested our help, as it was feared that there may be human remains buried there.

In the hallway, Holmes noticed a rug was slightly elevated in one part, and I helped him to roll it back. His instincts were right, since underneath the rug was a trap door. Dear reader, you could not guess what we found looking up at us from a room below. Thankfully, there were no human remains, but hundreds of stray dogs!

The owner of the property explained that things had gotten out of hand. Apparently, they had rescued a few stray dogs, but the dogs had bred and their numbers had increased dramatically. The dogs were removed for rehousing and were in good health, apart from needing a bath.

Relieved not to be dealing with a murder case, Holmes posed me this question on the way home:

"If there were 100 pairs of dogs and each pair had two pairs of pups, but sadly 25 pups died, how many animals did that leave in total?"

Can you figure it out?

The Need for Speed

Holmes and I joined the police in pursuit of an escaped convict. The word from the police was that the rogue was on his way to the City, about 4 miles from our current location.

All of the Hackney cabs were in use, and the trains were out of action that day, so our only option was to take a tram. The tram speeds and departure times were all a jumble to me, but Holmes thrived on sorting out the tangle of information.

Tram	Speed	Departs
1A	2 miles an hour	1:30
1B	4 miles an hour	2:40
1C	6 miles an hour	2:55

"Can you work out which tram would get us to the City in the quickest time?" Holmes asked.

Can you figure it out?

A Problem at the Pottery

Recently, Holmes and I were summoned to Stoke-on-Trent to investigate a series of despicable acts of vandalism to the precious China pots made in a factory there.

For several nights, we staked out the factory floor. There was not much to do, except to watch and wait. Holmes filled the time speculating on the number of pots that had been unfortunately destroyed. When he had exhausted that line of mental calculation, he then tested me with a number riddle:

"Think of a number, Watson, and double it. Then multiply your answer by four, and divide that answer by eight. What number do you end up with?"

We solved the crime on the third night. Astonishingly, the culprit was only a stray cat chasing some rats around the factory, smashing pots in the chase. Holmes advised the owners to block up the hole where the cat was gaining access and set traps to banish the rats.

But I still hadn't solved Holmes' number riddle. Can you answer it?

A Baby Brainteaser

Holmes and I were in attendance at a maternity hospital in Newcastle to deal with a rather distressing incident involving the kidnapping of a baby. Fortunately, the case was quickly resolved, when we discovered that an overly doting relative had merely taken the baby outside for some fresh air.

The sight of so many babies was still fresh in Holmes' mind on the journey home, and he could not resist testing me with a brainteaser.

"Two boys were born to the same mother on the same day, at the same time, in the same year, but they are not twins. How is this possible?" he asked.

I did not have a clue. Can you solve the riddle?

An Arctic Mission

One of the remotest and also the coldest places we have been summoned to was the Arctic. Scotland Yard had heard that Jake Parker, a notorious criminal, was on the run and hiding out in the Arctic. It amazes me what lengths criminals will resort to in order to escape the law!

Holmes and I were accompanied by an expert who had been on several polar expeditions previously. On arrival, we were informed that Parker had been seen 3 miles away, just over a snowy ridge.

We would require a team of five dogs to pull our sled over the frozen landscape. We just needed to select the five fastest dogs, based on the information on a sheet of paper. This was a riddle I was not prepared for when my fingers, nose, and toes were freezing over the longer we remained there.

Dasher: runs at 18 miles an hour.

Hunter: faster than Snowy, but slower than Sprite.

Sprite: 2 minutes slower than Star.

Snowy: 9 minutes slower than Polar.

Ice: takes 12 minutes to run 3 miles.

Bright: the slowest dog.

Polar: runs at 6 miles an hour slower than Dasher.

Star: runs 4 minutes slower than Dasher.

Can you calculate which are the five fastest dogs that we needed to pull our sled?

SOLUTIONS

CAUGHT RED-HANDED 4
Mary played chess with George.

CHASING OUR TAILS 5
Holmes was right as Moriarty was teasing them because roosters don't lay eggs, so the riddle held no clues to his whereabouts.

ALL ABOARD 6
The clues reveal that the criminal sat in either seat numbers 10 or 15. Earlier in his report, Watson mentioned that Holmes had arrested a male—"him"— so this rules out seat 10, meaning that the criminal sat in seat 15.

THE RIVER RIDDLE 7
The anaconda would be Watson's choice, since the anaconda won't be hungry as it goes for months in between meals.

A CASE OF DECORUM 8–9
The blackmailer was suspect three because they referred to Mrs. Flora Perkins as an "old lady," yet Holmes hadn't revealed this. So how did they know, if they had never met her?

IN HOT PURSUIT 10
Moriarty will be on the 7:11 train, which arrives at Glasgow first, at 5:26. The 7:08 arrives at 5:29, and the 7:21 arrives at 5:30.

AN AGE-OLD QUESTION 11
Mrs. Hudson is 40, and her grandfather is 80.

A TIMELY ESCAPE 12
It's bad luck to see a ginger cat when you're a mouse!

SOME SHAMELESS MUGGINGS 13
Holmes knew that the apothecary was lying because it was spring, and chestnut trees don't produce chestnuts until October.

THE PYRAMID PUZZLE 14
Net B cannot be made into a square-based pyramid.

TALKING IN RIDDLES 15
The day Watson had this conversation was January 1st, and Tommy's birthday is December 31st. Tommy was 13 the day before yesterday (December 30th), then turned 14 the next day. This year on December 31st, he'll turn 15, so next year he'll turn 16.

THE DOCKLANDS DILEMMA 16
Silence!

A BURNING QUESTION 17
Candle C has the most time left to burn, 2 hours 50 minutes, and is the candle Holmes would choose. Candle A has 1 hour 30 minutes of burning time left, and Candle B has 2 hours 40 minutes of burning time left.

RIVALRY BETWEEN SIBLINGS 18–19
Between them, Walter and Iris spent 90% of the time looking after their father, meaning that John spent 10% of the time, since the other two spent no time. If John was left 50 sovereigns, then that is 10% of the amount. So the whole amount of the father's fortune (100%) is 10 x 50 sovereigns, which is 500 sovereigns.

A RECTANGULAR PROBLEM 20
There are 18 rectangles.

A COAT CONUNDRUM 21
There is one raincoat, one fur coat, and one riding jacket.

THE LOST LOOT 22
east.

AN IRRITABLE INTERRUPTION 23
8 + 8 + 8 + 88 + 888 = 1,000

A DASTARDLY DOG-NAPPER 24
The numbers increase by 4 (23), then 5 (28), then 6 (34), then 7 (41) ... so the next number house will be 41 + 8 = 49.

A CODED MESSAGE 25
The code uses the first letter of each letter string to spell out each word—the number of letters in each letter string corresponds with the number of letters in each word. The letter reads: You will find the booty in an old suitcase at Baker Street lost property.

SPOT THE FAKE 26
Brooch 5 is the real brooch that belongs to Lady Morgan.

AN EYE FOR DETAIL 27
Suspect A is 12 inches wide and the only person narrower than 14 inches, and is therefore the thief. The other suspects are the following widths:
B = 18 inches; C = 15 inches; D = 18 inches; E = 20 inches.

THE SUSPICIOUS STALKER 28–29

The stalker is the opera singer. The musician and the opera singer are telling lies, the costume maker is telling the truth.

SOME LIGHT RELIEF 30

A bed!

READ ALL ABOUT IT 31

Holmes was smirking at the man's ignorant comment, because survivors would not be buried since they have survived.

THE CHIMNEY CONUNDRUM 32

Nets A and B can be made into a cylinder, net C cannot. The circles need to be on opposite sides of the rectangle to work.

A WET RIDDLE 33

No one under the umbrella got wet because it wasn't raining!

CONFUSION IN COURT 34

The fact that the accused man didn't look toward the door gave him away. He didn't look because he knew his wife was dead, because he had murdered her.

A FAMILY PUZZLE 35

Mrs. Hudson has seven nieces and one nephew from that sibling, since each of the nieces has the one brother.

THE DEVIOUS DECOY 36–37

The Moon!

A CRUMPLED CLUE 38

They need to head north.

A PUZZLING SEQUENCE 39

Box B comes next in the sequence. Starting with the smallest shape in the middle of each box, the sequence is: black triangle, white rectangle, black triangle, white rectangle ... black triangle. For the next biggest shape, the sequence is: circle, triangle, square, circle ... triangle. For the final shape, the sequence is: thick black square border, thick black square border, thin square border, thin square border ... thick black square border.

KICKING UP A STORM 40

Handyman one is the most expensive and is the crook: charging 40 shillings for the work (10 x 4) and 5,000 shillings for the tiles (500 x 10) = 5,040 shillings total. Handyman two is charging 28 shillings for the work (14 x 2) and 4,400 shillings for the tiles (440 x 10) = 4,428 shillings in total.

THE MISSING ABACUS 41

Alice Gilbert is lying, since she would not be copying down a poem in an arithmetic lesson—that would be in an English lesson. Alice Gilbert is the thief.

THE FATAL DROP 42
Holmes had to open all of the windows, meaning all the windows had been closed. If the victim had accidentally fallen out of an open window, and the crime scene had been left as it was found, that window would still be open.

THE SEAT MIX-UP 43
The seats should be as follows: Elizabeth: a forward-facing window seat; Sidney: a backward-facing aisle seat; Bert: a forward-facing aisle seat; Rachel: a backward-facing window seat.

CODED CLUE 44
Holmes abandoned the search because he had missed Moriarty. The message is in back-to-front mirror writing and reads: My dear Holmes, You may be the smartest detective, but you can't outwit me, as I'm the greatest criminal of all time. By the time you read this message, I will be long gone from here. Moriarty.

A DELICATE RIDDLE 45
A promise!

A COOKING CONUNDRUM 46
Mrs. Hudson has 1 ½ dozen eggs, which is 18 eggs (12 + 6). There are nine people: Mrs. Hudson, Watson, Holmes, five nieces, and one nephew. Two eggs per person means 18 eggs are required, so Mrs. Hudson has enough eggs.

A ROBBERY AT SEA 47
The sailor is lying and is the thief. The sailor said the flag was upside down, but the Japanese flag is a red circle on a white background, so it cannot be upside down because a circle is the same any way up.

A STICKY PROBLEM 48–49
The clues were that the gardener had leaves and twigs stuck all over his clothes, and he wore a sweet-smelling aftershave. Honey is sticky and sweet-smelling, so the gardener was most likely covered in honey! It was also suspicious that the gardener came over at the time they discovered the honey had been stolen, suggesting he that was nearby and may have just stolen the honey.

A RIDDLE IN THE RAIN 50
An umbrella.

GUESS THE NAME 51
The third child is Ebba.

THE MYSTERY PACKAGE 52

Delete the word *opera* after the first letter of each word. The letter reads: I am being blackmailed and need your help. Meet me backstage after this opera performance. With regards, Irene.

THE RIVER RIDDLE 53

The key to this puzzle is realizing that the woman can bring things back across the river.

There are the following two solutions:

1 Take the rabbit over.

2 The woman returns on her own.

3 Take the carrot over.

4 The woman returns with the rabbit.

5 Leave the rabbit back at the start, and take the fox over.

6 The woman returns on her own.

7 Take the rabbit over.

OR

1 Take the rabbit over.

2 The woman returns on her own.

3 Take the fox over.

4 The woman returns with the rabbit.

5 Leave the rabbit back at the start, and take the carrot over.

6 The woman returns on her own.

7 Take the rabbit over.

A COMMOTION IN THE KITCHEN 54

Mrs. Hudson had 10 jars (15 - 5). If each jar holds 1 pound, then 10 jars hold 10 pounds. If there are 16 ounces in 1 pound, then in 10 pounds there are 160 ounces (16 x 10). The 10 jars therefore hold 160 ounces of preserve If Mrs. Hudson has made 155 ounces of preserve, then she has enough jars.

A PERPLEXING PUZZLE 55

In the top row, the triangles change from two white triangles containing black triangles to two black triangles containing white triangles; a black rectangle containing a white circle to a white rectangle containing a black circle; two white squares containing white squares to two white squares. Using the same rules, the missing circle will have two white hexagons containing black circles in the top row; a white triangle containing a black triangle in the middle row; and two white squares in the bottom row. Therefore, the missing circle is C.

EVALUATING THE EVIDENCE 56–57

Holmes released John Grimes because he is innocent. A trusted Baker Street Irregular said that two of the suspects are telling the truth, and one is a liar. Therefore, Peter Price must be the liar, since he has accused both the other two suspects of lying, which is not possible. If John Grimes and Alice Parker are telling the truth, then Peter Price committed the crime.

A ROYAL RIDDLE 58

There were 21 pies in total. The Queen had eaten 11 pies (10½ (half of 21 + ½), leaving 10 on the platter.

A WELL-PLANNED ESCAPE 59

Professor Moriarty put on a disguise—there were lots of disguises because an actor lived in the house—and picked the lock. Then, when he saw the guard leave his post, he walked out of the door along the bridge. Before 10 minutes were up, he turned around and started to walk back toward the house. The guard returned to his post to see a man he didn't recognize approaching the house. He told the man that no visitors were allowed and sent the man (who was Moriarty) away.

A WORLDLY QUESTION 60

Greenland was still the biggest island in the world, even before it was discovered!

THE MISSING DOMINOES 61

A RACE AGAINST TIME 62

The heiress is hidden in the shed in the first column and first row.

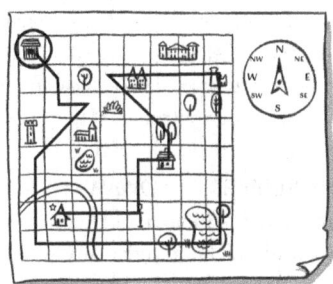

AN INVENTIVE MIND 63
A window!

THE DECIPHERING DETECTIVE 64
Monday is the name of a horse! The man walked into town and came back on a horse.

AN INVESTIGATION AT THE DOCKLANDS 65
Only Thomas Evans was a suspect, since according to the witness reports, only Thomas Evans was actually approaching the river. The other people were walking away.

A SLIPPERY THIEF 66–67
Mary Bright is telling the truth, and the other two keepers are lying. Mary is innocent, and one of the other keepers stole the penguin. Since they are both lying, the elephant keeper must have stolen the penguin.

AN ICY DISCOVERY 68
Watson is describing a glove.

SOME SHADY BUSINESS 69
One, two, and three. $1 + 2 + 3 = 6$ and $1 \times 2 \times 3 = 6$.

A SKITTLES SKIRMISH 70
Dorothy is the cheater.

A PREDICTABLE CASE 71
The score is always 0–0 before a game starts.

THE WINDOW MESSAGE 72
To work out the directions, swing the compass picture around, so that south is at the top, then make a half-turn clockwise (north), a quarter-turn counterclockwise (west), and a half-turn clockwise (east). Watson needs to head east.

A SMALL PIECE OF EVIDENCE 73
A good detective follows these procedures: Press any button, and wait a few minutes. Then press that same button again. Quickly press a second button. Open the door. If the light is on, then they know that the second button controls it. If the light is off, the detective feels the bulb (please note that it is not safe to touch a light bulb that may have been on, because it will be very hot—only a trained detective can do that). If the bulb is hot, then the first button pressed controls it. If the bulb is cold, then the third button (which has not been touched) controls it.

THE SLIPPERY STOWAWAY 74–75
Two weeks is 336 hours (14×24), meaning that the antelope was not in danger since it was an hour under two weeks.

THE BAFFLING EQUATION 76
Turn the equation upside down so it reads: 108 = 6 x 18.

THE CONFUSING CONVERSATION 77
There are four sisters (including Mrs. Hudson) and three brothers in Mrs. Hudson's family.

A NUMBER RIDDLE 78
11 and 88 each look the same backward and upside down.

THE DAILY RIDDLE 79
Percy does not have any brothers. He has two sisters who are both writers.

A PACKING PROBLEM 80
Watson needs 60 small boxes (6 crates) and 6 large boxes (1 crate), which is 7 crates.

A PERPLEXING CASE 81
Holmes believed that Victor Leonard had decorated the walls of the drawing room with wallpaper laced with the poison arsenic, which killed Beatrix Price. Beatrix began feeling unwell after Victor had re-papered the wall, so the poison must have been in the wallpaper, and it took a week of exposure to the poison to kill Beatrix Price. The police needed to send off a sample of wallpaper to a forensics expert, to prove it contained arsenic, which was also found in Beatrix's body. In Victorian times, arsenic was added to some paints on wallpaper designs to give brighter shades.

AN EVENING EMERGENCY 82
1 and 9. So the numbers to the combination are: 8, 9, 7, 2, 1, 9.

A MASTER OF DISGUISE 83
Moriarty's nephew's son's father's uncle is Moriarty!

THE CHICKEN COUNT 84–85
There should be 40 chickens and 30 nesting boxes.

A PROBLEM TO PONDER 86
65% are fish; 20% are frogs; 10% are newts; and 5% are water snails.

THE MISSING SQUARE 87
Square 2 is the missing square of D. Each rectangle in the corresponding position in the square to its right doubles the number of lines.

SHERLOCK'S BIGGEST FAN 88
They headed west: Start by facing north; then face south (turn 180°); then face east (turn 90° counterclockwise); and finally face west (turn 180°).

BOTHERSOME WEATHER 89
Suspect Three's boot print had pointed toes and no heel, showing that he was the pickpocket.

A RIOTOUS JOURNEY 90

Gentleman One and Gentleman Two contradict each other, so one is lying. Therefore, the lady is telling the truth, and Gentleman Two sat in the seat first.

EXAMINING THE EVIDENCE 91

The thief used the man's shoe to carry the coins, which could hold up to 15 pounds of coins ($375 \div 25 = 15$).

DOTTY ABOUT DICE 92–93

The highest numbers the dice could be are 5, 6, 5, and 6. Therefore, the highest total is: $5 + 6 + 5 + 6 = 22$.

THE SCHOOL SUSPECT 94

You give 39 children one slate, and you give the last child the box containing the slate.

A SENSELESS ATTACK 95

The answer to Moriarty's riddle is three. The group includes three people who are related: the grandfather (one person), who is a grandfather to the son here (one grandfather) and also a father to the father here (one father); the father (one person), who is also a son to the grandfather here (one son); and a father to the son here (a second father); the son (one person), who is a son to the father here (a second son).

A PROBLEM SHARED 96

Instead of giving an apple to each child because there were not enough, Holmes suggested that Mrs. Hudson make some apple crumble using the apples, sugar, flour, butter, and oats.

RIDDLE TIME 97

Sand. You can make sand castles on the beach; sand carried by wind or waves can erode mountains over time; you won't be able to see if you get sand in your eyes; glass is made out of sand.

A NOISY DISPUTE 98–99

There are only two feet, because cows and sheep have hooves, and a sheepdog has paws.

THE MYSTERIOUS POISONING 100

The poison was in the ice cubes. When Holmes and Watson drank the punch, it was cold because the ice was still frozen. The poison wasn't released into the punch until the ice cubes started melting, which was after Holmes and Watson had left.

AN EYEWITNESS ACCOUNT 101

The man in the suspect lineup who Nell Morgan picks out as the master forger is her butler.

THE BAKER STREET IRREGULARS 102
All of them, since a house can't jump!

THE MAGIC BEHIND THE TRICK 103
The volunteer's hand warmed up the coin. We know it was a wintery evening, so the other coins were cold. Mabel selected the warmest coin from the cup. Try it yourself!

THE BREAKFAST MEETING 104
Lunch and dinner!

RIDDLE WARS 105
A person on a horse!

A PRICING QUANDARY 106–107
A pear costs 1½ pennies (1½d). The other prices of the fruit are: apple—2d; blackberry—½d; gooseberry—1d; raspberry—1d; plum—1½d.

UNDER THE WEATHER 108
In 48 hours, it will still be midnight, so it will not be sunny because it will still be dark outside.

TROUBLE AT THE ZOO 109
A giraffe's shadow!

FEUDING FAMILIES 110
Nine years. It starts as 1 unit in height; in one year it will grow double this, which is 2 units; in the second year, double that will be 4 units; in year three, it will be 8 units; in year four, 16; in year five, 32; in year six, 64; in year seven, 128; in year eight, 256; in year nine, 512, and then its maximum height in the tenth year would be 1,024. Half of 1,024 is 512, which it grew to at nine years.

THE MYSTERIOUS ESCAPE 111
The man escaped through the window. He reached the window by standing on a block of ice, which had now melted. He would have gotten the ice from the icebox in the kitchen on the right.

A CANINE CONUNDRUM 112
100 pairs of dogs = 200 adult dogs. If each pair had two pairs of pups, then each pair had four pups, so there were 400 pups (100 x 4). The total of pups and adult dogs is 600 (400 + 200 (100 x 2)), minus the 25 dogs who didn't make it, which is 575 dogs in total.

THE NEED FOR SPEED 113
Tram 1A takes two hours to travel 4 miles, and arrives at 3:30; Tram 1B takes one hour to travel 4 miles and arrives at 3:40; Tram 1C takes 40 minutes to travel 4 miles and arrives at 3:35. Tram 1A arrives first and gets them to their destination the quickest.

A PROBLEM AT THE POTTERY 114
You end up with the same number that you started with. If a number is doubled and multiplied by four, it's actually been multiplied by eight, so dividing by eight will always give you the number you started with.

A BABY BRAINTEASER 115
The babies are two babies from a set of triplets!

AN ARCTIC MISSION 116–117
You need to calculate how long it would take each dog to pull the sled 3 miles. It would take the following times: Ice: 12 minutes; Dasher: 10 minutes (18 miles ÷ 3 miles = 6; 60 minutes ÷ 6 = 10 minutes); Star: 14 minutes; Polar: 15 minutes (12 miles ÷ 3 miles = 4; 60 minutes ÷ 4 = 15 minutes); Snowy: 24 minutes; Sprite 16 minutes; Hunter: sixth fastest; Bright: the slowest. The five fastest dogs are Dasher, followed by Ice, then Star, then Polar, then Sprite.